THE KIPPAH

MOSAICA PRESS

ALL ABOUT YARMULKES, JUDAISM & LIFE

RABBI MOSHE BECKER

Mosaica Press, Inc.

Designed and typeset by Daniella Kirsch

ISBN-10: 1-937887-69-3
ISBN-13: 978-1-937887-69-8

Published and distributed by:
Mosaica Press, Inc.
www.mosaicapress.com
info@mosaicapress.com

In Loving Memory of

Henry Leibovici, M.D.

הרצל בן אברהם

May 19th, 1937 – April 16, 2002

נלב"ע ד' אייר תשס"ב

Beloved Father, Grandfather, and Doctor

My father carried himself like a kippah carries a man — upwards.

He was a caring and knowledgeable medical doctor, an honorable husband, a model of a father, a playful grandfather, and a supportive father-in-law.

He started from a very humble existence in Romania; his mother passed away when he was young and his father was unschooled.

Although faced with these obstacles and more, he built himself a flourishing medical practice and a large family.

As busy as he was throughout his life, he always instilled an appreciation of Judaism into his three sons, who in turn instill even more Judaism into their children.

In Memory of

Mr. Samuel Haber

שמחה בן צבי הירש

נלב״ע ה׳ סיון תשע״ה

FOREWORD

The kippah is a very familiar head covering known to both Jews and Gentiles alike. Throughout history, Jews have been known as the "People of the Book," yet we have no book written exclusively about kippahs! This was my question — a question which originated generations ago when my family was Torah observant. Unfortunately, with pogroms, the Holocaust, and modernity, my family went from grandparents who were very observant and knowledgeable about Judaism to grandchildren who were much less so.

We are bringing back what was lost in our family by instilling Judaism in our children. However, before we can do that, we must first instill those teachings in ourselves. I started by reading books by Rabbi Aryeh Kaplan about *tzitzis* and *tefilin* and naturally began wearing them. When I searched and asked for a book about kippahs I found that one did not exist.

In addition, as a practicing physician in a hospital, I noticed that I was more efficient in every way and was happier at work with the kippah. I was also more thoughtful towards my wife and children (aka builders). Was this little reminder the cause of these changes at work and home? I was directed to Rabbi Yaacov Haber and together we were able to put together this book. That is the story on the surface.

The miracle underneath is that I was blessed with the idea of this book. There have been hundreds of millions of Jews who have existed in this world and among them thankfully countless brilliant Torah scholars. How could a Jew with so little knowledge of Torah be able to ask a question that was never asked? Much less likely, be a part of this project and surrounded by such great Torah scholars? Could wearing a kippah be such a basic tenet that the commonality made it elusive? Without question, the grandiosity of the kippah is in the free will of those who wear it, rather than in Torah or Rabbinic law. That free will was given by G-d, which answers all the questions above.

That being the case, all the profits of this book will go to *tzedakah* as verified by Rabbi Yaacov Haber, and mandated by the sole sponsor of this book. And, as I am taught by many Rabbis, I challenge G-d to repay to you the kindness you have performed by buying this book.

With all blessings and every success,

Samuel Leibovici, M.D.

ACKNOWLEDGMENTS

It is the mark of an educated mind to be able to entertain a thought without accepting it.

– Aristotle

The above quote captures the difficulty associated with writing about an item that is familiar to most readers. In all likelihood, readers of this book either already wear yarmulkes or do not. Most of us are taught at a very young age one way or the other regarding wearing a yarmulke. It is challenging to think objectively about this most ubiquitous aspect of Jewish attire and life, about which many of us have long since formed our attitudes.

One can never thank one's parents fully or adequately. My parents, Rabbi Dr. Ephraim and Mrs. Malka Becker, taught me to wear a yarmulke at all times and to never be ashamed of it. I took my yarmulke for granted as a child, even while living in Wisconsin, where yarmulkes were not especially common. My yarmulke was truly a reflection of what we were taught at home: living as a Jew means something at all times and in all places. My parents have been an incredible source of inspiration and encouragement in all my learning, teaching, and writing.

I have been fortunate over the past several years to study with and give classes to a wide range of audiences at the Jewish Renaissance Experience in Scarsdale, NY and at the Young Israel of White Plains. Much of the material in this book was assembled in the context of these classes, and it is to the participants in all these classes that I am eternally grateful for providing me the opportunity to develop my thoughts on the yarmulke and many other topics.

The immediate impetus for the writing of this book came from a very special couple, Dr. Samuel and Danielle Leibovici, of Norfolk, VA. Dr. Leibovici is a yarmulke wearer where few such individuals exist, and he has "acquired" this *mitzvah* as his own. Commissioning the writing and publishing of this book is a beautiful expansion of his connection to this *mitzvah*, enabling others, those who do wear yarmulkes as well as those who do not, to better appreciate the importance and significance of wearing a yarmulke. In addition to sponsoring this volume, Dr. and Mrs. Leibovici provided crucial guidance and perspective on our topic. I am deeply grateful to them for creating this opportunity.

The entire team at Mosaica Press was instrumental in the production of this book, most notably Rabbi Yaacov Haber and Rabbi Doron Kornbluth. I thank them, along with their team of editors, graphic designers, and support staff for all their hard work and dedication to this project.

Special recognition is due to my father-in-law, Rabbi Yaacov Haber, who has been a mentor, role model, and ongoing inspiration to me. I thank him not only for encouraging me to take on the writing of this book, but also for everything I have learned from him. He and my mother-in-law, Mrs. Bayle Haber, are grandparents par excellence to my children, and I thank them both for all their support and encouragement through this and all my other efforts.

Although they were not directly involved in this work, I must note the contributions of my teachers, in this context specifically Rabbi Yitzchak Berkovits and Rabbi Meir Triebitz of Jerusalem. These dedicated and brilliant teachers helped develop my approach to understanding Halachah, *Aggadah*, and the relationship between these areas of Torah. As such, their guidance greatly impacted this book.

I thank my children for their mostly indirect and involuntary involvement in this book. While they certainly gave up time with me to allow for this project to happen, having children also reminds us that some of the most important aspects of Jewish continuity and connection are not clear-cut Halachic obligations. Wearing a yarmulke is one such important example.

This project would never have been successful if not for the constant support of my wife, Ester Malka. Thank you for your endless love, support, and partnership.

Finally, thank you to our Creator for blessing us with His Torah, our pathway to connection with His infinite wisdom. G-d sustains us constantly, providing our material needs as well as feeding our souls with the beauty and depth of Torah. I feel deeply blessed to be able to share with others some of the Torah I learned.

I pray that this short book will increase understanding of the yarmulke while also introducing some readers to the process of Torah study and Halachic ruling, thereby sanctifying the name of G-d and His Torah.

Moshe Becker
November 2015

PREFACE

Our local Hebrew Academy of Tidewater once forfeited a game of basketball because the referee wouldn't allow them to play ball with their yarmulkes. Their conviction made the paper, but it also inspired one eighth grader to begin wearing his yarmulke all day. He had noticed that the boys with yarmulkes always made the most impressive shots.

When I was a young boy in Buffalo, NY, I was one of a handful of boys who wouldn't walk four steps without a yarmulke. My classmates would take advantage of my limitations and grab my yarmulke for a game of "kippah-way" while I stood helpless on the sidelines.

One day I went home and cried. My father shared with me that in his day he was the only boy his age in Buffalo with a yarmulke. Even his teachers would politely remind him to remove his kippah. Keeping that kippah on was tough, but it made him strong. That kippah would never come off.

My father made me feel good about my yarmulke. He also gave me some father-to-son strategy. The next day in school I didn't just stand there with my hand on my head. I reached nonchalantly into my right pocket and took out a backup yarmulke. I walked away smugly while my oblivious friends continued to hoot and toss the kippah to and fro.

I had a third yarmulke in my left pocket, but I never needed it. I don't know whether my friends felt like losers because they had been outsmarted or they began to respect my conviction. I do know that they never played "kippah-way" again. When Rosh Hashanah came they asked for forgiveness and we all ended up a little bit smarter.

We get more questions and comments about our yarmulkes than about anything else we do. It is a visible manifestation of our unwavering and proud belief in a Higher Power, our constant reminder that we are not the top of the totem pole.

Last month, as Hurricane Joaquin made its way to Norfolk, I found myself at an outdoor ATM making a deposit in thirty-five-mile-per-hour winds. Nearby, a woman in a parked car watched me intently. Afraid that I had offended her in some way, I finished my transaction and walked over to her car to ask if I could be of assistance. "Yes," she said, "I've been watching you stand outdoors in a hurricane for five minutes, and not once has your little hat blown off of your head. Please tell me how you do it!"

I'm not sure how we do it, but we do. Jews around the world and through generations have managed to proudly wear that yarmulke through the most trying of circumstances and the most difficult storms. We don't just wear the yarmulke when we pray. We wear it to work, to the bank, to basketball games, and in hurricanes. It shapes who we are and inspires others to be more aware of G-d's constant presence in our lives.

Congratulations to my good friends the Leibovicis for spearheading and embracing this project. I join them in a prayer that this book will be an effective vehicle to share the concept of the yarmulke — its depth, its history, and its laws — with an ever-broadening audience.

Rabbi Sender Haber
Congregation B'nai Israel
Norfolk, VA

INTRODUCTION

What is a yarmulke?

Yarmulke (YAR-mal-ka) is the term often used to refer to the small round cap worn by Jewish men. Other often-used words are kippah (*ki-PAH*), *koppel*, or skullcap. A yarmulke may be black, white, or multicolored and can be made out of any material. Some common versions are: a black velvet deep bowl shape; a similarly shaped but colorful type, knitted out of yarn; a small knitted version; and a flat leather or suede variation.

Virtually all Orthodox Jewish men wear a yarmulke, although it is not uncommon for one to remove his yarmulke while at work.[1] In Conservative communities, men wear head coverings during services and while

1 This will be discussed later on in greater detail.

attending Jewish functions, and some wear one at all times.[2] In most Reform congregations today, although the matter of head covering is a personal choice, many do wear head coverings for Jewish activities, such as prayer, study or a funeral.[3]

But the yarmulke is more than just an article of clothing. The yarmulke, perhaps more than anything else, is the symbol of a Jew. In many circles it is the only distinctive garment that sets the Jew apart from his Gentile friends, neighbors and colleagues. We may take this symbol for granted, but let's take a moment to consider the following questions: Is a yarmulke absolutely required? What does it signify? Why is it so important? Is it ever acceptable to remove the yarmulke from one's head?

A quick look through the Torah or a list of the 613 *mitzvot* will not yield a commandment to wear a yarmulke. This

---

2 Later in this work, we discuss the traditional distinction between men and women regarding head coverings. We do not address the relatively recent development in some communities for women to don yarmulkes, which is worthy of a separate study.

3 The current state of affairs represents a shift from the classical Reform position. In its early days, many Reform leaders insisted on abolishing the head covering during services. In fact, in many Reform Temples the errant visitor wearing a yarmulke would be asked to remove the offending headgear. For additional background, see Y. Rivkind, "תשובת הרב אריה מודינה על גילוי הראש", in *Sefer Ha-Yovel l'Levi Ginsburg*, New York, 1946, pp. 402–403 and n. 2 in particular.

widely observed feature of Jewish life is not mentioned in the Mishnah either. While the Talmud does mention the concept, it does not treat head covering as an obligation. In fact, as we'll see shortly, the Talmud seems to indicate the contrary!

The purpose of this work is to shed some light on these questions. Hopefully, the reader will gain an understanding of the yarmulke by exploring some classical sources on the topic. We will discover a wide range of views among the Halachic authorities regarding the severity of wearing a yarmulke and if and when one is permitted to go bareheaded.[4]

Before we proceed, a few words are in order regarding the words "kippah" and "yarmulke." These terms do not appear in earlier rabbinic sources, where no unique noun is associated with a head covering. Kippah is a modern usage of the Hebrew word for a round cap; it is also used to refer to the arc of a domed structure, a fitting way to describe the traditional small head coverings Jewish men wear. Defining the term "yarmulke," used for several generations in Ashkenazi communities, is more difficult.

---

4 This work is a brief overview of the matter and not intended as a comprehensive review of all available literature on head coverings. The interested reader is directed to the recently published *Otzar Hakippa* (Jerusalem, 2014) by A.D. Wasserman, an encyclopedia of material pertaining to yarmulkes and hats in Halachah and Jewish tradition.

A popular explanation is that the term is a conjugation of ירא מלכא, meaning "to fear the King." This reflects the idea we'll see shortly that the purpose of the yarmulke is to heighten one's awareness of G-d. Another suggestion is that the term originates from Turkish; either *Yağmurluk*, which means rain gear, or a combination of *yarim*, half, and *qap*, hat.[5] Whatever the name, we'll explore later on whether a unique, dedicated hat such as a yarmulke is required or any covering suffices.

We open with the following story, an instance of extreme sacrifice for the sake of a yarmulke:

> The year was 1838. After a lengthy trial, R' Pinchas Shapiro and R' Shmuel Abbe Shapiro, grandsons of the great R' Pinchas of Koritz and owners of the Slavuta printing press, were convicted of murder and sentenced to receive five hundred *speisrutten* each. The *speisrutten* were administered as follows: the accused was tied to a rifle on each side and led between two rows of soldiers, each of whom would strike the convict as he was led past. Five hundred *speisrutten*

5 See W. Gunther Plaut, "The Origin of The Word 'Yarmulke,'" in *Hebrew Union College Annual*, Vol. 26, (1955), pp. 567–570 for various possible explanations of the term.

meant that the victim passed two rows of 250 soldiers on each side to receive five hundred beatings — one from each soldier.

The brothers had been accused of arranging for the murder of one of their employees — who had in fact committed suicide — as well as using their printing press to print subversive anti-Tsar material. Proof was never produced to substantiate either allegation, but the matter was ultimately handed over to the military court. It was the military court that issued the sentence of the *speisrutten*, a punishment usually administered to soldiers. By all accounts, these older, distinguished individuals were not expected to survive such severe punishment.

At one point, as the two brothers were led through the rows of soldiers, R' Pinchas' yarmulke fell off his head. He could not bend down to retrieve it as he was tied and bound, so he stopped walking. As he stood there, the blows continued to rain down on his back, yet he refused to budge. Only when the soldiers leading him picked up his yarmulke and placed it back on his head did R' Pinchas continue walking. To such an extent R' Pinchas felt it was necessary to

> wear a yarmulke under all circumstances, that he endured extra beatings so as not to walk with his head uncovered.

Although this story attests to R' Pinchas' fortitude and saintliness, we record it here not simply to remember his devotion, but to highlight the extreme importance that the yarmulke has attained in Jewish life and practice. Many Jewish men since R' Pinchas Shapiro have made their own unique sacrifices, in one form or another, to keep their yarmulkes. It is our hope that this book will provide some insight into that commitment.

Technically, I am told, I could use anything to cover my head. A hat. A turban. A bandana. A cat (just joking, animal lovers — relax!). Whatever.

I choose to wear a yarmulke.

Kind of surprising, since I'm Protestant.

Just kidding — I'm Jewish.

Still, kind of surprising, since I'm kind of....how shall I say this?...inconsistent in my Jewish observance. In other words, if I wanted an excuse not to wear one, I could certainly find one.

So why do I choose to stand out as a Jew?

Because I want to stand out as a Jew.

Our family is kind of blonde (Russian Jews — go figure). So, anyway, we don't "look Jewish," whatever that means.

Never bothered my parents. Growing up in Communist Russia, I guess that was an advantage for them, actually. For my sister and me, growing up in the USA, it was different. We wanted to stand out. She wears a Star of David necklace and I wear a kippah.

We are proud Jews — and we want people to know it.

D.M.

CHAPTER 1

The Torah makes no mention of a requirement for all men to wear a head covering, explicitly or even implicitly.[6] Yet, often more than any other single action, a man's decision to discard his yarmulke may be seen as his official break from his community. Conversely, choosing to wear a yarmulke when one previously did not can be a major positive statement of commitment.

Why is this so?

---

6 Regarding married women there is reference to the need for a head covering, as expressed in the portion dealing with the *Sotah*. See *Bamidbar* 5:18: "וְהֶעֱמִיד הַכֹּהֵן אֶת הָאִשָּׁה לִפְנֵי יְהוָה וּפָרַע אֶת רֹאשׁ הָאִשָּׁה וְנָתַן עַל כַּפֶּיהָ אֵת מִנְחַת הַזִּכָּרוֹן מִנְחַת קְנָאֹת הִוא וּבְיַד הַכֹּהֵן יִהְיוּ מֵי הַמָּרִים הַמְאָרְרִים — And the priest shall set the woman before G-d, and uncover the woman's head, and put the meal-offering of memorial in her hands, which is the meal-offering of jealousy; and the priest shall have in his hand the water of bitterness that causes the curse."

Indeed, the Torah makes no mention of a general obligation for men to cover their heads. However, special hats are prescribed for the *Kohanim* as part of their unique priestly garb. Moreover, the hats, called *Migbaot*, are designed to be לכבוד ולתפארת, for honor and beauty.[7] The honor and glory is not intended just for the *Kohanim* as individuals, but rather to highlight and glorify what the *Kohanim* represent: service of the Holy One in His holy place. So, the Torah does not require anyone but the *Kohanim* while they are serving in the Temple to wear hats, but that very instruction teaches us that a hat can be worn as a sign of respect, honor, and dignity, both for its wearer and for what the wearer represents. Let's keep this in mind as we explore further.

In the Talmud we find several references to head coverings and to the men who wore them. These discussions in the Talmud form the bedrock of our analysis of the yarmulke. Let's take a look at them now:

BABYLONIAN TALMUD, *SHABBAT* 118B:

אמר רב הונא בריה דרב יהושע תיתי לי דלא סגינא ד׳ אמות בגילוי הראש.

---

7 *Shemos* 28:40: "וְלִבְנֵי אַהֲרֹן תַּעֲשֶׂה כֻתֳּנֹת וְעָשִׂיתָ לָהֶם אַבְנֵטִים וּמִגְבָּעוֹת תַּעֲשֶׂה לָהֶם לְכָבוֹד וּלְתִפְאָרֶת — And for Aaron's sons you shall make tunics, and you shall make for them girdles, and you shall make hats for them, for honor and beauty."

> R' Huna, the son of R' Yehoshua said: "I will merit because I did not walk four cubits with a bare head."

In this statement we see the head covering described as a praiseworthy practice. It is so meritorious that R' Huna is careful to not even walk a few feet with a bare head!

Of course, our immediate reaction to this passage should be to conclude that a head covering is not a requirement. If it were an obligation, to which everyone is expected to adhere, why should R' Huna take particular pride that he covers his head? Clearly, neither R' Huna nor the Talmud by quoting him felt that a head covering at all times is obligatory.

> BABYLONIAN TALMUD, *KIDDUSHIN* 31A:
>
> רב הונא בריה דרב יהושע לא מסגי ארבע אמות בגילוי הראש אמר שכינה למעלה מראשי.
>
> R' Huna the son of R' Yehoshua would not walk four cubits with a bare head. He used to say, "The Divine Presence is above my head."

This statement too is particular to R' Huna and also makes no mention of an obligation for all to follow R' Huna's practice. However, here we are given a reason that could be applicable to everyone: one covers his head because the

Divine Presence is above at all times. Missing is an explanation of the association between a head covering and the Divine Presence.

R' Yechiel Michel Epstein, a major Halachic authority of the late nineteenth century, explains that our heads hold our brain, which is the most G-d-like aspect of a human.[8] We need to remind ourselves that we are but human, and in comparison to G-d our intellect is limited. We thus cover our heads as a sign of humility and submission in G-d's presence.

We'll now look at another passage from the Talmud that refers to head coverings.

BABYLONIAN TALMUD, *KIDDUSHIN* 8A:

כי הא דרב כהנא שקיל סודרא מבי פדיון הבן אמר ליה לדידי חזי לי חמש סלעים אמר רב אשי לא אמרן אלא כגון רב כהנא דגברא רבה הוא ומבעי ליה סודרא ארישיה אבל כולי עלמא לא.

Such as R' Kahana, who would take a hat from the home of a *pidyon haben*. He said "To me it is

8 R' Yechiel Michel Halevi Epstein (Belarus, 1829–1908) in *Aruch HaShulchan* 2:10:

והענין שהראש שבו המוח, שהוא מקור החכמה והיראה – אין לו להתגלות לפניו יתברך שמלא כל הארץ כבודו, כמו שאין לעמוד במקום קדוש בגילוי ראש. ואם אינו עושה כן, עזות יצרו מתגבר עליו גם בלא הרגשה

See page 82 for English translation.

worth five *selaim*." R' Ashi said: "This is only said with regard to someone like R' Kahana, who is a great man and needs a hat upon his head, but not with respect to everyone else."

A firstborn son must be redeemed from a *Kohen* by his parents in exchange for five *selaim* (the value of 100 grams or 3.5 oz of silver).[9] R' Kahana was a *Kohen*, and at one *pidyon haben* accepted a hat in lieu of five *selaim*. This is legitimate because an object of value can be substituted for the required currency. The Talmud, however, limits any further applicability of this practice; R' Kahana was unique because he was an important person and needed to cover his head. A hat therefore carries value for R' Kahana, while a regular person, who is not in such need of a hat, would not be allowed to substitute the normally required five *selaim* with a hat.

So, while this passage also teaches the significance of a head covering, it concludes that covering one's head is not a required practice for all. R' Kahana, as a major Torah scholar, was required to cover his head, but individuals of lesser status are clearly not obligated to do so.

---

9 *Bamidbar* 18:16: "וּפְדוּיָו, מִבֶּן-חֹדֶשׁ תִּפְדֶּה, בְּעֶרְכְּךָ, כֶּסֶף חֲמֵשֶׁת שְׁקָלִים בְּשֶׁקֶל הַקֹּדֶשׁ: עֶשְׂרִים גֵּרָה, הוּא — And their redemption, money, from a month old shalt thou redeem them...shall be, according to thy valuation, five shekels of silver, after the shekel of the sanctuary...the same is twenty *gerahs*."

Another Talmudic figure, R' Yehoshua ben Levi, wouldn't go out to the street with a bare head, even when he was in a rush.

> BABYLONIAN TALMUD, *KIDDUSHIN* 30A:
>
> רבי חייא בר אבא אשכחיה לריב״ל דשדי דיסנא ארישיה, וקא ממטי ליה לינוקא לבי כנישתא. א״ל: מאי כולי האי? א״ל: מי זוטר מאי דכתיב: ״והודעתם לבניך״ וסמיך ליה ״יום אשר עמדת לפני ה׳ אלהיך בחורב״.
>
> R' Chiya ben Abba found R' Yehoshua ben Levi wearing a plain cloth upon his head and taking a child to the synagogue [for study]. "What is the meaning of all this?" he demanded. "Is it then a small thing," he [R' Yehoshua] replied, "that it is written, 'And thou shalt make them known to your sons and your sons' sons, which follows, 'That is the day that thou stood before the Lord thy G-d in Horeb.'"[10]

Rashi explains that "What is the meaning of all this?" was directed at the "plain cloth" on R' Yehoshua ben Levi's head.[11] R' Chiya was surprised to see R' Yehoshua

---

10 *Devarim* 4:9.

11 R' Shlomo Yitzchaki (France, 1040–1105) is the primary commentary on the Babylonian Talmud.

ben Levi in the street with an unbecoming head covering. R' Yehoshua ben Levi replied that he was rushing to take the child to his studies so he stuck the first available head covering on his head so not to go bareheaded.[12] This passage, however, can easily be understood in light of the previous passage. Just as R' Kahana was somewhat unique due to his stature, so too was R' Yehoshua ben Levi of similar status. R' Yehoshua ben Levi thus had to find something, even a simple cloth, to put on his head before going out.

In another Talmudic passage, we see a broader expectation to wear a head covering:

> BABYLONIAN TALMUD, *KIDDUSHIN* 29B:
> משתבח ליה רב חסדא לרב הונא בדרב המנונא דאדם גדול הוא א"ל כשיבא לידך הביאהו לידי כי אתא חזייה דלא פריס סודרא א"ל מאי טעמא לא פריסת סודרא א"ל דלא נסיבנא אהדרינהו לאפיה מיניה א"ל חזי דלא חזית להו לאפי עד דנסבת.
>
> R' Chisda praised R' Hamnuna before R' Huna as a great man. Said he to him, "When he visits you, bring him to me." When he arrived, he saw that he wore no [head] covering. "Why have

12 Rashi, ד"ה דשדי דיסנא ארישיה and ד"ה מאי כולי האי.

> you no head-dress?" asked he. "Because I am not married," was the reply. Thereupon he [R' Huna] turned his face away from him. "See to it that you do not appear before me [again] before you are married," said he.

R' Hamnuna is chastised for being unmarried, and R' Huna refuses to speak to him further until he marries. In this case, although R' Hamnuna's lack of a head covering was cause enough to raise questions, ultimately R' Huna's chief criticism was of R' Hamnuna's marital status. It appears that his justification for not wearing a head covering — that he was unmarried — was itself a legitimate answer.

We turn to another story in the Talmud, which in concept seems to support an even broader use of head coverings:

> BABYLONIAN TALMUD, *SHABBAT* 156B:
>
> דאימיה דר"נ בר יצחק אמרי לה כלדאי בריך גנבא הוה לא שבקתיה גלויי רישיה אמרה ליה כסי רישיך כי היכי דתיהוו עלך אימתא דשמיא ובעי רחמי לא הוה ידע אמאי קאמרה ליה יומא חד יתיב קא גריס תותי דיקלא נפל גלימא מעילויה רישיה דלי עיניה חזא לדיקלא אלמיה יצריה סליק פסקיה לקיבורא בשיניה.
>
> R' Nahman ben Isaac's mother was told by astrologers: Your son will be a thief. [So] she did

> not let him [be] bareheaded, saying to him, "Cover your head so that the fear of Heaven may be upon you, and pray [for mercy]." Now, he did not know why she spoke that to him. One day he was sitting and studying under a palm tree and his garment fell off his head; temptation overcame him, he climbed up and bit off a cluster [of dates] with his teeth.

R' Nachman ben Yitzchak's mother warned him to keep his head covered so that he should maintain his fear of Heaven. This story is about an individual and a mother who was fearful for her son's future, but the Talmud makes it clear that wearing a head covering assists in maintaining fear of Heaven. Of course, it also clearly does not mandate head covering as an obligation.

The following Talmudic passages are critical of those who fail to cover their heads:

> BABYLONIAN TALMUD, *KIDDUSHIN* 33A:
>
> רבינא הוה יתיב קמיה דר׳ ירמיה מדיפתי חלף ההוא גברא קמיה ולא מיכסי רישא אמר כמה חציף הא גברא א״ל דלמא ממתא מחסיא ניהו דגיסי בה רבנן.
>
> Ravina was sitting before R' Yirmiya of Difti and a man passed by with his head bared. Ravina said

> "How insolent is this man!" R' Yirmiya replied "Perhaps he is from Matta Mechasia, where they are used to being in the presence of Rabbis."
>
> *MASECHET KALLAH* AND *KALLAH RABBATI* 2:2:
>
> פעם אחת היו זקנים יושבים, עברו לפניהם שני תינוקות, אחד גלה את ראשו, ואחד כסה את ראשו, זה שגלה ראשו, ר׳ אליעזר אומר ממזר, ר׳ יהושע אומר בן הנדה, ר׳ עקיבא אומר ממזר ובן הנדה.
>
> On one occasion, the elders were sitting while two children passed by. One child bared his head and one covered his head. With regard to the one who bared his head, R' Eliezer said "He is a *mamzer*"; R' Yehoshua said "He was conceived by a *niddah*"; R' Akiva said "He is both a *mamzer* and conceived by a *niddah*."

The child's audacity was so clear that it led the *Tannaim* to assume that something must be significantly wrong with his lineage. The *Beraitah* goes on to describe how further investigation proved R' Akiva's assessment to be correct.

The above sources all speak in praise of the head covering or in criticism of those who do not cover their heads.[13]

---

13 At least in the presence of rabbinic figures.

Clearly the Talmud considers head covering a meritorious practice that perhaps Torah scholars are required to follow, but nowhere does it state that head covering is an obligation for all men. In fact, nearly all the passages quoted above are from Aggadic stories in the Talmud. While the Aggadic sections of the Talmud teach us important lessons, normative practice is generally learned from the direct Halachic instructions of the Talmud.

We do find some reference to head covering in Halachic sections of the Talmud — in the context of saying prayers, blessings, and *Shema*. It is commonly understood that for the activities named one must wear a yarmulke. As we'll see, the Talmudic sources are not entirely clear on this matter either. We'll turn to these discussions now.

In the next passage, the Talmud associates each of the morning blessings with an activity that one does while preparing for a new day:

BABYLONIAN TALMUD, *BRACHOT* 60B:

כי מתער אומר אלהי נשמה שנתת בי טהורה... כי שמע קול תרנגולא לימא ברוך אשר נתן לשכוי בינה להבחין בין יום ובין לילה כי פתח עיניה לימא ברוך פוקח עורים כי תריץ ויתיב לימא ברוך מתיר אסורים כי לביש לימא ברוך מלביש ערומים כי זקיף לימא ברוך זוקף כפופים כי נחית לארעא לימא ברוך רוקע הארץ על המים כי מסגי לימא ברוך המכין

מצעדי גבר כי סיים מסאניה לימא ברוך שעשה לי כל צרכי
כי אסר המייניה לימא ברוך אוזר ישראל בגבורה כי פריס
סודרא על רישיה לימא ברוך עוטר ישראל בתפארה...

When he awakens he should say "My G-d, the soul you placed in me is pure." When he hears the sound of the rooster, he should say "Blessed Who has given understanding to differentiate between day and night." When he opens his eyes, he should say "Blessed Who has given sight to the blind." When he sits up he should say "Blessed Who has released the bound." When he dresses he should say "Blessed Who clothes the naked." When he stands up he should say "Blessed Who straightened the bent." When he places his feet upon the ground he should say "Blessed Who has spread the earth over the water." When he walks he should say "Blessed Who firms man's footsteps." When he ties his shoes he should say "Blessed Who provides all my needs." When he tightens his belt he should say "Blessed Who girds Israel with strength." When he places a covering on his head he should say "Blessed Who adorns Israel with glory."

Our custom differs in practice; we recite all the blessings at once before the prayers and not with their associated activities as listed. Nevertheless, several conclusions can be drawn from the passage above. First, it is assumed that one covers his head as a matter of course. A blessing is designated, as part of each man's morning routine, for placing his hat on his head. R' Yosef Karo, in his *Beit Yosef*,[14] explains that we say a *brachah* when putting on a hat because it's a *mitzvah* that's incumbent upon all Jews.[15] Hence the wording of the blessing "who adorns Israel with glory."[16] To support this statement, the Beit Yosef quotes a passage from the *Zohar*. We will return to the latter shortly.

It is also assumed that one recites all the earlier blessings without a head covering! In the passage quoted above, the blessing recited when donning a head covering is last in a list of morning activities and their related

---

14 R' Yosef Karo (Spain; Israel 1488–1575) in his commentary on *Tur, Orach Chaim* 46. R' Karo is often referred to as "the Beit Yosef" after his work of the same name. Note that we'll establish below that according to the Beit Yosef there is in fact a requirement to wear a head covering at all times.

15 Later we will address the possible difference between men and women in this respect.

16 Note that this is the same word used in the Torah to describe the hats of the *Kohanim*.

blessings. Not only does the individual go some time without a head covering, he even says a number of blessings before covering his head. If it is absolutely necessary to cover one's head when saying blessings, how could he recite all the earlier blessings with his head bare?

Perhaps the above passage in *Brachot* follows the view of the Mishnah in *Megillah* and *Masechet Soferim*,[17] which are among the few early sources to address praying and reciting blessings with one's head uncovered. Let's take a look:

> MISHNAH, *MEGILLAH* 4:6:
>
> קטן קורא בתורה ומתרגם, אבל אינו פורס על שמע, ואינו עובר לפני התיבה, ואינו נושא את כפיו. פוחח פורס את שמע ומתרגם, אבל אינו קורא בתורה ואינו עובר לפני התבה ואינו נושא את כפיו..
>
> A minor may read the Torah and translate, but he may not lead the blessings of *Shema*, nor may he go before the Ark (to lead the repetition of the silent prayer), nor may he lift his hands (for the *Kohen's* blessing). A *poche'ach* may lead the blessings of *Shema* and he may translate (the Torah), but he may not read the Torah, nor go before the Ark nor lift his hands.

---

17 Another of the "Small Tractates" mentioned earlier.

The *poche'ach* in the Mishnah is allowed to recite blessings, but he cannot lead the congregation in certain communal aspects of the service because his appearance is undignified.

What is a *poche'ach*?

Fortunately, he is described in more detail in a parallel text in *Masechet Soferim*:

MASECHET SOFERIM 14:15:

קטן קורא בתורה ומתרגם... פוחח הנראים כרעיו או בגדיו ערומי' או מי שראשו מגולה פורס את שמע ויש אומרי' בכרעיו ובגדיו ערומים פורס אבל לא בראשו מגולה — אינו רשאי להוציא הזכר' מפיו. בין כך ובין כך מתרגם אבל אינו קורא בתורה ואינו עובר לפני התיבה ואינו נושא את כפיו:

A minor may read from the Torah and translate... A *poche'ach*, whose legs can be seen or his clothes are tattered or whose head is uncovered, may lead the blessings of the *Shema*. Some say: If his legs can be seen or his clothes are tattered he may lead the blessings of *Shema*, but not if his head is uncovered — he may not mention G-d's name. Either way, he may translate, but may not read from the Torah, nor go before the Ark, nor raise his hands.

A *poche'ach* is defined here as someone who is not properly attired, including one whose head is bare. Although that is largely considered an obstacle to his leading the communal services, here in *Masechet Soferim* we see a disagreement whether or not one whose head is uncovered may mention G-d's name at all. The Mishnah in *Megillah*, unlike the passage in *Masechet Soferim*, does not suggest any distinctions between different types of *poche'ach*, hence it's reasonable to understand that the Mishnah adopts the first view we read here in *Masechet Soferim* — that a *poche'ach* includes someone whose head is bare. Thus, in ruling that a *poche'ach* is only disqualified from leading the services, the Mishnah apparently rules that one may recite a blessing even with his head uncovered. It would further seem reasonable that the Talmud in *Brachot* also follows this view, allowing one to recite all the morning blessings up to "He who adorns Israel with glory" without a head covering.[18]

A *Midrash*, also discussing *Shema*, seems to support the view that no special conditions, including a head covering, are necessary for one to fulfill the Torah obligation of reciting *Shema*:

---

18 As noted above, we do not have the custom of reciting the blessings in this manner at all.

MIDRASH RABBAH EMOR (*PARSHAH* 27, 6):

אמר הקדוש ברוך הוא לישראל: הדא פרוסדוגמא דידי לא הטרחתי עליכם ולא אמרתי אליכם שתהא קורין ק"ש לא עומדין על רגליכם ולא פורעין את ראשיכם, אלא (דברים ו): בשבתך בביתך ובלכתך בדרך ובשכבך ובקומך.

The Holy One Blessed be He said to Israel: "Behold I have not burdened you with My declaration and I did not say that you must recite the *Shema* standing on your feet nor with a wrapping around your heads."[19] Rather: "When you are sitting in your house and walking on your way; when you lie down and when you rise."

To summarize, in our Halachic texts from the Mishnah and Talmud we see that one is generally expected to wear a head covering. One whose head is uncovered is not considered fit to lead the prayer services in many capacities. However, we still have not seen a text explicitly requiring that one wear a head covering at all times. In fact, we have

---

19 The Hebrew words ולא פורעין את ראשיכם are problematic in this and other texts. For a complete analysis and justification of our translation, see M. Kasher "חילופי מנהגים בענין גילוי הראש" in *Horeb* 4:7–8 (1937) pp. 195–206. Linguistic difficulties notwithstanding, the Beis Yosef, Vilna Gaon, and others all quote this *Midrash* as support that a head covering is not required even for *Shema* and blessings.

found that, at least according to some, one may even recite blessings and the *Shema* with a bare head!

We're not quite ready to give up yet on an early source for the yarmulke. True, we don't see an explicit instruction in the Mishnah and Talmud to cover one's head, but reference to such a requirement can be found in the *Zohar:*

> *ZOHAR, PARSHAT V'ETCHANAN* (260:2):
>
> תא חזי מאן דקאים בצלותא בעי לכוונא רגלוי ואוקמוה ובעי לחפיא רישיה כמאן דקאים קמי מלכא ובע ילמכסייה (נ״א לאסתמא) עינוי בגין דלא יסתכל בשכינתא
>
> Behold, one who stands in prayer must hold his feet together and he must cover his head in the manner that one stands before a king. And he must close his eyes so that he does not look at the Divine Presence.

Finally we read an explicit and direct instruction to cover our heads for prayer!

> *ZOHAR, RAAYA MEHEMNA III* 187:
>
> פתח ואמר (קהלת ב׳, י״ד) החכם עיניו בראשו וגו׳ וכי באן אתר עינוי דבר נש אלא בראשו דילמא בגופו או בדרועיה דאפיק לחכם יתיר מכל בני עלמא. אלא קרא הכי הוא ודאי דתנן לא יהך בר נש בגלוי דרישא ד׳ אמות. מאי טעמא דשכינתא שריא

על רישיה וכל חכים עינוי ומלוי בראשו אינון בההוא דשריא וקיימא על רישיה וכד עינוי תמן לינדע דההוא נהורא דאדליק על רישיה אצטריך למשחא בגין דגופא דבר נש איהו פתילה ונהורא אדליק לעילא ושלמה מלכא צווח ואמר (שם ט) ושמן על ראשך אל יחסר דהא נהורא דבראשו אצטריך למשחא ואינון עובדין טבאן ועל דא החכם עיניו בראשו.

It says: "The wise man's eyes are in his head" (Eccl. II, 14). Where, it may be asked, should they be if not in his head? What it means, however, is this: We have learnt that a man should not go four cubits with his head uncovered, the reason being that the *Shechinah* rests on the head. Now a wise man's eyes are directed to his head, to that which rests on his head, and then he knows that the light which is kindled on his head requires oil, which consists of good deeds, and therefore the eyes of a wise man are towards his head, and no other place.

Here, for the first time, we see a need for all men to wear a head covering at all times. We're also given a reason and imagery to help understand the requirement: The *Shechinah* rests on one's head, as represented by the imaginary candle that's burning there. This candle must be fueled by good deeds. Wearing a yarmulke presumably will remind the "wise person" to keep his "eyes directed at his head" and ensure that he continues to fuel the candle with good deeds.

And finally, in a more extreme statement, the *Zohar* goes further:

> *ZOHAR, NASSO* 122B:
>
> אתמר כי על כל מוצא פי יי׳ יחיה האדם והיא על רישיה דב״נ... ובגין דאיהי על רישיה דב״נ אסיר ליה לב״נ למיזל ד׳ אמות בגלוי דרישא דאם היא אסלקת מעל רישיה דב״נ מיד אסתלקו חיים מניה.
>
> The verse states "For by that which departs the mouth of G-d does man live" and this is upon the head of man... And because it is upon man's head one is forbidden to walk four *amot* with a bare head, for if it is removed from his head, immediately his life will depart from him.

This is a difficult passage, and the meaning of "if it is removed from his head" in the final sentence may be unclear, but the *Zohar* states that is it forbidden to walk four *amot* with a bare head. This is the most severe statement we've seen thus far.

To summarize, we've seen many sources from Mishnah, Babylonian Talmud, *Midrash* and *Zohar*. In some of these sources we read laudatory comments about those who cover their heads, and in others criticism of those who do not. We discovered that while one cannot be a *shaliach tzibbur* — a representative to lead the communal prayer — with a bare head, the Mishnah does allow him to recite the prayers for himself. Finally, we saw mystical references in the *Zohar* to an absolute need for head covering.

Where does this leave us? Have we seen enough to understand R' Pinchas' commitment to the yarmulke expressed in our opening story? In the following pages we continue to explore some possible approaches.

I never really wanted to wear a kippah until I couldn't.

Part of my personality, I guess. I've always been a little counter-cultural, anti-establishment, and had problems with authority. School was hard for me, but life has been great.

In my family growing up, we only wore kippahs in synagogue on the rare occasions we would attend. We were Jewish but didn't wear it on our sleeves, so to speak — or on our heads.

Recently, I needed to visit Paris for business. My mother went crazy: it's too dangerous. They are killing Jews there... don't go... can't you use Skype?

So I did a little research.

Indeed, France has become dangerous for Jews.

Just consider some examples (unfortunately, not an exhaustive list) from the last three years: A Jewish school in Toulouse was attacked and four people were killed, including three children, with many injured. Four people were killed in an attack at a kosher supermarket in Paris. Three men were stabbed at a Jewish community center in Nice. A couple was attacked and robbed because "Jews always have money."

In other words, though I hate to admit it, Mom was right. No wonder so many French Jews are moving to Israel.

Still, if a person avoids all Jewish establishments and doesn't wear any identifying Jewish garb, there is little chance that he will be targeted. Indeed, the Chief Rabbi of France has told the community to wear baseball caps or other head-coverings instead of a kippah in any (even possibly) problematic areas.

I followed his directive, of course. And I know it is important to be safe.

However, I made it a point of pride to wear a kippah in 'safer' areas, such as the financial district and tourist sites. Jews have a right to self-identify as Jews. In the modern world, if we don't (carefully) exercise that right, we'll lose it. I never wanted to wear a kippah as much as when I wasn't supposed to wear one.

J.A.

CHAPTER 2

When it comes to deciding on matters of Halachah and validating our communal practices, it is insufficient to look at the Talmudic sources. The words of *Chazal*[20], as expressed in these texts, are the critical foundation indeed, but we always turn to the *Rishonim*[21] to interpret the Talmudic texts and then to the *Shulchan Aruch* for practical rulings. The *Rishonim* are the ones who would tell us which of the sources we've seen above supersede others and how we should resolve possibly conflicting sources.

---

20 "*Chazal*" is an acronym for "*Chachamenu Zichronam L'vracha*," our Rabbis of blessed memory.

21 Medieval commentators and Halachic authorities, such as Maimonides and others.

Here we'll take a look at a few passages from the *Rishonim* to give us a sense of how they perceived the matter of the yarmulke.

> *SEFER HAYIRAH OF RABBENU YONAH:*[22]
>
> ומעת קומו להתהלך על הדרך, יכפוף קומתו וישוח ראשו, כי השכינה למעלה מראשו, ולכן נכון לכסות ראשו, ואל יהיה בגילוי-ראש.
>
> From the moment he stands to go about his way he should lower his head, for the Divine Presence is above his head. Therefore it is appropriate to cover his head, and he should not be bareheaded.

Rabbenu Yonah stops short of suggesting that there is an absolute obligation for one to cover his head, but he ties head covering to the prohibition against "walking with an upright bearing", which is forbidden because it is an expression of arrogance. Covering one's head is a subset of not conducting oneself arrogantly, which is an absolute requirement. These two associated obligations, says Rabbenu Yonah, are relevant equally to all people and at all times.

---

22 Rabbenu Yonah of Gerona (Spain, d. 1263) was a leading figure of the Spanish community in his time. He was a disciple of R' Shlomo of Montpellier, one of the French *Tosafists*.

Rambam[23] discusses the head covering in several different contexts. Let us take a look at his words:

> *MISHNAH TORAH, HILCHOT DEIOT* 5:6:
>
> צניעות גדולה נוהגים תלמידי חכמים בעצמן לא יתבזו ולא יתגלו ראשן ולא גופן
>
> Torah Sages conduct themselves with exceptional modesty. They do not demean themselves and do not bare their heads or their bodies.

> *MOREH NEVUCHIM*, III CH. 52:
>
> והוא שאנו תמיד לפניו יתעלה, הולכים ובאים בנוכחות שכינתו. גדולי החכמים ז״ל היו סולדים מלגלות את ראשיהם כי השכינה אופפת את האדם
>
> We are always before God, and it is in the presence of His glory that we go to and fro. The great men among our Sages would not uncover their heads because they believed that God's glory was around them and over them.

In both quotes from Rambam's writings we read that great Torah Sages do not bare their heads because they recognize that G-d's presence is upon them. Rambam is

---

23 Maimonides; R' Moshe ben Maimon (Spain; Egypt; d. 1204).

informing us that covering one's head is meritorious — a trademark of a *talmid chacham*. Perhaps he's suggesting that everyone adopt the practice, but he does not require it.

On the other hand, we also hear a different voice in the *Rishonim*:

> *KOL BO, SIMAN* 11 AND *ORCHOT CHAYIM, SIMAN* 1:48:[24]
>
> וכתב הר״מ נ״ע שאינו אסור לילך בגלוי ראש כי מה שאמרו בפרק כל כתבי הקדש תיתי לי דלא סגינא ד׳ אמות בגלוי ראש ר״ל שזו מדת חסידות והר״ף כתב שיש למחות שלא ליכנס בבית הכנסת בגלוי ראש.
>
> R' Meir wrote that there is no prohibition to walk with a bare head,[25] for that which is quoted in *Perek Kol Kitvei*, "I will merit because I do not walk four *amot* with a bare head" is intended to teach us that this is a pious practice. Rabbenu[26] wrote that we should

---

24 The author of the *Kol Bo* and *Orchot Chayim* is R' Aharon HaKohen of Narbonne, France. He lived in the 13th and 14th centuries and emigrated to Majorca when the Jews were expelled from France in 1306.

25 Referring to the famous Maharam of Rothenberg, who died in 1305 and was a major leader of the community in his generation. He was one of the latest of the *Baalei Hatosafot* and his influence therefore remained strong throughout subsequent generations.

26 Rabbenu Peretz was one of the French Tosafists during the second half of the 13th century.

prevent people from entering the Synagogue with a bare head.

R' Meir, known to many as the Maharam of Rothenberg or just Maharam, held that there is no obligation to cover one's head on a constant basis. However, perhaps we can infer from Maharam's words that in his time it was customary for Jews to cover their heads. We'll return to this point shortly.

Another important quote in the *Kol Bo* is the statement of Rabbenu Peretz that one should not enter a synagogue with a bare head.

A similar, but more direct statement is made by another one of the *Rishonim*. In the context of proper preparation for reciting *Birkat Hamazon*, Rabbenu Yerucham writes:[27]

TOLDOT ADAM V'CHAVA, NETIV 16, CH. 7:

שנותן סודר על ראשו שאסור לברך בגלוי הראש

He should place a cloth upon his head, for it is forbidden to say *brachot* with a bare head.

Here, too, we can infer that it was accepted and acceptable to go bareheaded at some times, but Rabbenu

27 Rabbenu Yerucham lived in the 14th century and was originally from Provence, but later moved to Spain and studied under the Rosh.

Yerucham states conclusively that while reciting blessings and praying it is absolutely forbidden to be bareheaded. He seems to be ruling in accordance with the view in *Masechet Soferim* that forbids all prayer with a bare head,[28] and with the *Zohar* which states that one must cover one's head for prayer.[29]

To summarize, we've seen samplings of the views of the *Rishonim* on the matter of wearing a yarmulke. They range from the view that one must always cover his head to the opinion that one may not be bareheaded while saying prayers or blessings and when in a Synagogue, but at other times and places there is no requirement whatsoever. For a middle position we saw Rambam, who describes head covering as the practice of great Torah scholars, and maybe something we should all emulate.

Why does the existence of Jews bother so many people?

The United Nations has more resolutions against Israel than Sudan, North Korea, and a dozen other murderous tyrannical regimes — combined. Are you kidding?

Why is it that a Christian or Muslim or Buddhist or Hindu or whatever can walk down the street

28 See second source on page 37.

29 See first source on page 40.

anywhere in Europe — wearing whatever religious garb they want — without a problem, but it is simply dangerous for identified Jews to walk around many European cities today? Don't blame it on the Middle East — a similar situation existed seventy-five years ago, one hundred years ago, and many hundreds of years ago.

Anti-Semitism is crazy. While there are, of course, many millions — billions, actually — of wonderful people on the planet, there is a significant number who, generation after generation, society after society, simply don't like Jews. Whether we are rich or poor, powerful or powerless, integrated or marginalized, religious or secular... whatever.

I wear a kippah for me — to remind myself of who I am and motivate myself to be a better, more spiritual person.

But I also wear a kippah for the world — society has to get comfortable with the existence of minorities and Jews in particular. If we hide who we are, what hope is there?

D.B.

CHAPTER 3

We've seen several sources that teach the value of wearing a head covering. We learned that some say one must wear a yarmulke at all times. The next step is to consult the *Shulchan Aruch*, the Code of Jewish Law.[30] If in fact there is an obligation to wear a yarmulke, we expect to find this obligation set forth clearly in the *Shulchan Aruch*.

---

30 *Shulchan Aruch* (lit. 'A Set Table') is the Code of Jewish Law, authored by R' Yosef Karo (Spain; Safed, 1488–1575). It is considered to represent the consensus and binding ruling on most matters of Jewish practice and ritual. R' Yosef Karo's rulings are supplemented by glosses of R' Moshe Isserles in instances where the customs of the Ashekanazic communities of Poland and Germany differed from those practiced in the Sephardic countries such as Spain, Egypt, Morocco etc.

To properly understand what we find in the *Shulchan Aruch* it will be helpful to first see a few passages in an earlier code, commonly known as the *Tur.*[31] R' Yosef Karo, when writing the *Shulchan Aruch*, followed the structure and subdivisions of the *Tur*. In addition, prior to writing the *Shulchan Aruch*, R' Yosef Karo also wrote a separate commentary on the *Tur*, called *Beit Yosef*, in which he explores much of the background to the Tur's rulings. His comments in the *Beit Yosef* are particularly relevant to our discussion about yarmulke. We cited briefly from the Beit Yosef above; below we'll examine his views regarding the obligation to wear a yarmulke altogether.

In the following pages we'll look at the various rulings in the *Tur*, the *Shulchan Aruch*, and their commentaries pertaining to covering one's head. We'll discover that nearly everyone agrees that a head covering is required — at least at certain times.

---

31 *Tur* is the popular name for the book named *Arba'ah Turim*, which is a predecessor to the *Shulchan Aruch*. The author of the *Tur* was Rabbi Yaakov ben Rabbenu Asher, though he is often referred to by the name of his book simply as "The Tur." He lived from the mid-13th to the mid-14th century. *Arba'ah Turim* literally means "four pillars," referring to the four sections the author divided all areas of Jewish conduct into: *Orach Chaim*, Laws of Daily Life; *Yoreh Deah*, Laws of Rituals; *Even Haezer*, Laws of Marriage and Divorce; *Choshen Mishpat*, Laws Governing Finance. This four-part division was followed by *Shulchan Aruch* and many subsequent authors as well.

The Tur describes some features of appropriate general conduct:

> *TUR, ORACH CHAIM* 2:
>
> ויקום וילך בכפיפת קומה, כדאיתא פרק קמא דקידושין: ״אמר רבי יהושע בן לוי: אסור לילך בקומה זקופה, שנאמר: מלא כל הארץ כבודו״. ויכסה ראשו, כדאיתא נמי התם: ״רב הונא לא אזיל ארבע אמות בגילוי הראש. אמר: שכינה למעלה מראשי״.
>
> One should rise and walk with a slightly inclined posture, as is stated in the first chapter of *Kiddushin*. R' Yehoshua ben Levi said: "It is forbidden to walk with an upright posture, for the verse states, 'The earth is filled with His honor.'" And he should cover his head, as it further states there, "'R' Huna would not walk four *amot* with an uncovered head, saying 'the Divine Presence is upon my head.'"

The Tur reads R' Huna's statement from *Kiddushin*,[32] which we saw earlier, as guidance for each of us. The Tur surely was aware that a simple read of the Talmud in *Kiddushin* implies that there is no requirement to wear a yarmulke and wearing one was a practice that was unique to R' Huna. Evidently, the Tur felt that by telling us about

32 See second source on page 25.

R' Huna's meritorious custom, the Talmud is instructing us to learn from R' Huna, internalize the message of being aware of the Divine Presence, and follow in his footsteps. The purpose of the passage in the Talmud is not to tell a nice story about R' Huna, rather to convey an important lesson to the readers. In that vein, the Talmud relates this lesson as a story, and not simply as a law, so we understand that wearing a head covering is not just a mandate or wardrobe choice but a mindset we're supposed to live with constantly.[33]

The Tur mentions head covering in two other instances and the commentaries differ on how to understand the relationship between the various statements of the Tur. Let's take a careful look at these:

> *TUR, ORACH CHAIM* 8:
>
> ודרך העטיפה, רוחבה לקומת האיש, ומחזיר ב׳ ציציות לפניו וב׳ ציציות לאחריו, שיהא מסובב במצוות, ומכסה ראשו, שלא יהא בגילוי הראש, ויברך ״להתעטף בציצית״.
>
> The manner of wrapping (the *tallit*) is with its width wrapped along the height of the person;

---

33 For a complete analysis of the Tur's comment here, see the commentary of the Bach (*Bayit Chadash*, by R' Yoel Sirkis, who lived in Poland, 1561–1640) as well as the gloss of R' Moshe Isserles (Poland, 1520–1572) in *Darkei Moshe* ad loc.

> he should place two of the *tzitzit* corners in front of him and two in back, so he will be surrounded with the *mitzvot*. And he should cover his head, so his head should not be bare, and say the *brachah* "to wrap with the *tzitzit*."

How would you interpret the Tur's words "And he should cover his head so his should not be bare"? Does the Tur assume that the person's head was entirely bare up to this point, or does he simply mean that the individual must cover his head with the *tallit*, over and above whatever had been on his head previously?

The Tur's commentators disagree on this very point:

> *BEIT YOSEF, ORACH CHAIM* 8:
>
> ונראה דלאו למימרא שיכסה ראשו כדי שלא יהא בגילוי הראש לגמרי, שאין זה מעניין מצוַת ציצית; ועוד, דהיאך הלך לעשות צרכיו וליטול ידיו בגילוי הראש? אלא היינו לומר, שאף על פי שראשו מכוסה, דרך צנועים להטיל סודר או טלית על ראשם, וכדאיתא בשלהי פרק קמא דקידושין... לכך כתב שיכסה ראשו בטליתו, כדי שלא יהא בגילוי ראש מסודר או טלית, שדרך ליתן על כיסוי התחתון שבראש.
>
> ואפשר דהכי קאמר: יכסה ראשו בעניין שלא יהא בגילוי ראש מטלית של מצווה, שצריך שיכסה ראשו בציצית, לקיים מצוַת ציצית מן המובחר.

> It appears that this is not to say that he should cover his head so his head should not be entirely bare, for this is not related to the topic of *tzitzit*. Furthermore, how could he have gone to relieve himself and to wash his hands with a bare head? Rather, the intention is that even though his head is covered, it is the custom of pious people to cover their head with an additional covering, or with the *tallit*, as we see in the end of the first Chapter of *Kiddushin*... Therefore he writes that one should cover his head with the *tallit* so he should not be bare of the covering that is customary to place above the lower hat that is on his head already. Perhaps he means to say that one should cover his head such that it is not bare of the *tallit* of *mitzvah*. Thus his head will be covered with the [garment of] *tzitzit* and he thus fulfills the *mitzvah* in the ideal fashion.

As we can see, the Beit Yosef takes for granted that a yarmulke must be worn. In his understanding, since it goes without saying that the individual's head is covered, the Tur must be telling us that the person should cover his head specifically with the *tallit*, either because pious people wear an additional covering over their yarmulke or as an enhancement to the *mitzvah* of *tallit*.[34]

R' Moshe Isserles, another commentator, reads the *Tur* differently, though he prefaces with an important comment:

DARKEI MOSHE, ORACH CHAIM SIMAN 8:

ואף כי מצווה לשמוע אל דברי בית יוסף ופירושו, מכל מקום נראה לי שמה שכתב הטור: ״ומכסה ראשו כדי שלא יהא בגילוי הראש״ – הוא כפשוטו, כי בלא ציצית אין איסור לילך בגילוי הראש רק ממידת חסידות, כמו שכתבתי לעיל סימן ב׳ בשם הר״מ. ולכן כתב דבשעת עטיפת ציצית צריך לכסות ראשו.

It is a *mitzvah* to adhere to the words of the Beit Yosef and his explanation. Nevertheless, it appears to me that the Tur wrote "And he should cover his head so as to not to be bareheaded" to be understood simply. For setting aside the *mitzvah* of *tzitzit* there is no prohibition against going bareheaded, rather it is a custom of the righteous, as I wrote earlier in *Siman* 2 in the name of Maharam. Therefore the Tur wrote that while wrapping the *tallit* one must cover his head.

---

34 The Beit Yosef invokes as proof the story from *Kiddushin* 29b (source on page 29) and states again that "obviously" even single men would not go bareheaded in the times of the Talmud.

We read above that Maharam (R' Meir of Rothenberg) was of the opinion that a yarmulke is not required at all times.[35] R' Moshe Isserles, in the passage just cited, follows the view of Maharam. He therefore reads the Tur's ruling literally and sees no need to explain the Tur in the novel way we read about in the *Beit Yosef*. Since it's perfectly possible and legitimate that an individual may not be wearing a yarmulke the Tur tells him that when donning his *tallit* he should cover his head.

Significantly, R' Moshe Isserles opens his remarks with "It is a *mitzvah* to adhere to the words of the Beit Yosef." R' Moshe Isserles disagrees with the Beit Yosef in thousands of cases. Why would he qualify his own opinion with a disclaimer that one should follow the Beit Yosef? It seems that practically and substantially R' Moshe Isserles did agree that one should wear a yarmulke. Though he disagreed with the Beit Yosef over the correct analysis of the Tur's words, he wanted the reader to know that he did not disagree with the value expressed in the *Beit Yosef*.

Let us get back to the *Tur*. If in fact one is not obligated to wear a yarmulke, as R' Moshe Isserles maintains, why does the *Tur* require a head covering while one is wrapping his *tallit*? For that we turn to our final quote from the *Tur*.

---

35 See first source on page 49.

TUR, ORACH CHAIM SIMAN 91:

בגדיו כיצד... ויכסה ראשו

How should his garments be (for prayer)? ... And he should cover his head.

Here, too, the Tur requires a head covering and does not go into any further detail or explanation. The Tur's commentators explain that this ruling follows the view of Rabbenu Yerucham that one is not allowed to recite any blessings or prayers with a bare head.[36] As we explained above, this view conforms to one of the opinions in *Masechet Soferim*. Apparently the Tur rules in accordance with that opinion and one therefore must cover his head for prayers and blessings.

In light of this last quote from the Tur, we can understand why he required above that one cover his head when donning the *tallit*. The very next thing the Tur says after describing the manner of wrapping the *tallit* is that the *brachah* "to wrap with the *tzitzit*" must be said. As we see now, one may only say a *brachah* if his head is covered. According to the understanding of R' Moshe Isserles, the person may very well have been bareheaded up to this point and now he needs to cover his head before saying a blessing. The Beit Yosef, on the other hand, insists that

36 See source on page 50.

the person should have been wearing a head covering anyway. He therefore explains that in the laws of donning the *tallit,* the Tur is referring to an additional head covering—above and beyond the yarmulke.

We've seen thus far from these passages in the *Tur* and its commentaries that it is forbidden to say a *brachah* with a bare head. Everyone seems to be in agreement on this point. However, while the Beit Yosef understood that one must always cover his head, R' Moshe Isserles maintains the view of Maharam and others that there is no requirement outside of prayer and the synagogue. He does, however, acknowledge the "pious trait" of wearing a yarmulke at all times and even said that it's a "*mitzvah* to follow the words of the Beit Yosef."[37]

The Beit Yosef himself codified all these rulings in his *Shulchan Aruch*, as we'll see presently. It is interesting to note that in none of these instances does R' Moshe Isserles comment or disagree despite the disagreement we saw above.[38]

---

37 In his words "מידת חסידות".

38 R' Yosef Karo wrote his commentary *Beit Yosef* on the *Tur* and R' Moshe Isserless (Rema) wrote his *Darkei Moshe* primarily to highlight and give authority to views that either diverge from those presented by the Tur and Beit Yosef or that were not recorded by them at all. The views of R' Yosef Karo and R' Moshe Isserless were set forth as independent codes

SHULCHAN ARUCH, ORACH CHAIM 2:

אסור לילך בקומה זקופה, ולא ילך ארבע אמות בגילוי הראש

It is forbidden to walk with an upright posture and he should not walk four *amot* with a bare head.

This ruling corresponds directly with the Tur's similar expression. We recall that the Tur gave as his reason the passage in *Kiddushin* describing R' Huna's practice of wearing a head covering.

In the laws of the *tallit* however, the ruling in the *Shulchan Aruch* is framed differently. First, we are taught the blessing, then, R' Yosef Karo tells us how we should wrap the *tallit* and wear it. Finally he concludes:

SHULCHAN ARUCH, ORACH CHAIM 8:

...ונכון שיכסה ראשו בטלית.

[...and] it is proper to cover his head with the *tallit*.

This statement has nothing to do with our discussion about yarmulkes! True to his own position, the author of

---

in the *Shulchan Aruch*, where R' Moshe Issereles's comments are recorded only where they differ from the primary text written by R' Yosef Karo. In our case, we would expect to find a disagreement in the *Shulchan Aruch* to mirror their different interpretations of the *Tur*.

the *Shulchan Aruch* had no reason to tell us anything about regular head coverings here. That ruling is given earlier, as we just read, and is an established assumption at this point. What is added here is the lesson that it is proper to cover one's head with the *tallit* — as an enhancement to one's fulfillment of the *mitzvah* of *tzitzit*.

Later on, in the laws of prayer, the *Shulchan Aruch* is straightforward when it comes to proper attire:

> *SHULCHAN ARUCH, ORACH CHAIM* 91:
> יש אומרים שאסור להוציא אזכרה מפיו בראש מגולה ויש אומרים שיש למחות שלא ליכנס בבית הכנסת בגלוי הראש
> There are those who say that it is forbidden to say G-d's name with a bare head. And there are those who say that we should object to people entering the synagogue with a bare head.

These two statements derive from the views of Rabbenu Yerucham and Rabbenu Peretz mentioned earlier. Of course, for R' Yosef Karo these views are essentially unnecessary as he holds that everyone must wear a yarmulke at all times regardless![39]

---

39 Methodologically, the *Shulchan Aruch* always introduces laws as "There are those who say..." if the given law is not found in the *Rambam*, *Rif*, or *Rosh*. This is not indication that he disagrees with the ruling in any

We've seen that according to the *Shulchan Aruch* one must wear a yarmulke when saying blessings, and one should wear a yarmulke at all times when walking more than four *amot*. Although R' Moshe Isserles expressed in *Darkei Moshe* that he felt the letter of the law did not require a yarmulke at all times, he does not present this view in the *Shulchan Aruch* and lets R' Yosef Karo's words stand.

Consequently, the basic ruling of the *Shulchan Aruch* is that one should wear a yarmulke at all times when walking more than four *amot* and one must wear a yarmulke for blessing and prayers even while sitting at home.

That Jews look different is not a new phenomenon or one invented by the Nazis. Indeed, Pope Innocent III declared at the Fourth Lateran Council in 1215:

"In several provinces, a difference in vestment distinguishes the Jews from the Christians; but in others, the confusion has reached such proportions that a difference can no longer be perceived. We order that the Jews of both sexes, in all Christian lands and at all times, shall be publicly

---

way. Perhaps the author especially wishes to qualify here, as the ruling would appear unnecessary if one follows his earlier ruling that a yarmulke must be worn always.

differentiated from the rest of the population by the quality of their garment."

Personally, I don't mind looking different. I am different. I don't believe in Christianity or Islam. Technology and openness are great, but I don't believe Western society is the be-all and end-all — take a look at what messages we are bombarded with, day after day.

Deep down, I know Judaism is full of beauty and truth. I'm Jewish, and proud to show it.

G.S.

CHAPTER 4

Thus far we have learned that the *Shulchan Aruch* instructs us to wear a yarmulke at all times. R' Huna is a role model whose practice of wearing a head covering we must emulate. As we saw in the various passages in the Talmud and *Zohar*, a yarmulke helps the wearer remember G-d's constant presence.

Additionally, one must cover his head for prayers and blessings. This is based on the ruling in *Masechet Soferim* that one may not even mention G-d's name with a bare head. So much so, that Rabbenu Peretz ruled that we should stop someone from entering a synagogue with his head uncovered.

Two of the commentators on the *Shulchan Aruch* questioned the basis for the blanket ruling that one must wear a yarmulke. After all, as noted above, the passages in the Talmud are not expressed as binding obligations for all. Furthermore, recall the *Midrash* that takes pride that the *mitzvah* of *Shema* can be fulfilled without special fanfare and does not require a head covering.[40] This is incompatible with the ruling that one absolutely must cover his head anytime he mentions G-d's name. How do we reconcile the sources?

In addressing these difficulties, the commentaries introduce completely new perspectives on the practice of wearing a head covering. As we will see, both approaches, though very different, are important for us, as they are directly relevant.

We won't see their complete analysis of the topic here. The interested reader is encouraged to study the original sources in their entirety. We will take a look at the conclusions of the Vilna Gaon[41] and the Taz,[42] respectively.

The Vilna Gaon, characteristically, briefly cites virtually every reference to the topic found in the Talmud, *Midrash* and *Zohar*. In his usual fashion, he reads these sources at face value and reaches the following conclusion:

---

40 See first source on page 49.

41 R' Eliyahu b. Shlomo of Vilna, known as the Gra or Vilna Gaon (Lithuania, 1720-1797).

42 Taz is an acronym for *Turei Zahav*, the commentary on *Shulchan Aruch* written by R' David Segal Halevi (Poland, 1586-1667).

BIUR HAGRA, ORACH CHAIM 8

כללא דמילתא אין איסור כלל בראש מגולה לעולם רק לפני הגדולים וכן בעת התפלה אז נכון הדבר מצד המוסר ושאר היום לקדושים שעומדים לפני ה׳ תמיד:

The summary of the matter is: There is no prohibition whatsoever to uncover one's head at any time. Only in the presence of important people and while praying it is proper and correct. At all other times, only those holy people who are always standing before G-d.

The Vilna Gaon requires only important people to wear a head covering. Additionally, he advocates that it is appropriate to wear a head covering while in the presence of important people. Even during prayer, study and while saying blessings it is proper and correct, but not obligatory. For all other people, at all other times, there is no problem whatsoever with going bareheaded.

This is consistent with his reading of the passages in the Talmud. Let's review: The Talmud extolls the virtues of wearing a head covering and stresses its ability to bring a person to greater connection with G-d, and perhaps there is an implicit recommendation that everyone should wear a yarmulke. However an actual requirement is only discussed with regard to important people. As we saw in one such example, R' Kahana could collect a hat in lieu of *five selaim* for *pidyon haben*, for he required a head covering due to his stature. The Vilna Gaon in turn rules that an important person must wear a head covering. As demonstrated above, the Mishnah rules that a *poche'ach* is allowed to recite prayers and blessings though his head is bare. Hence the Vilna Gaon rules that there is no obligation to wear a hat or yarmulke even for prayers. By the same token, it is clear from the same Mishnah that it is more respectful to cover one's head while praying. Therefore, the Vilna Gaon states that it is proper to do so, though not obligatory. Likewise, we saw the strong criticism of those who would remain bareheaded in the presence of the Rabbis. The Vilna Gaon says that it is appropriate, out of respect and deference, to wear a head covering in the presence of important people.

The Vilna Gaon thus rules, somewhat radically, that there is no obligation to wear a yarmulke at any time for most people![43]

---

43 A similarly minded, though somewhat more moderate version of this approach can be found in the *Responsa Maharshal* by R' Shlomo Luria (Poland, 16th century), chapter 72: "ולולי שאינני רגיל לחלוק על הקדמונים א"ל שיש גדול שיסייעני הייתי נוטה להקל ולברך בגילוי הראש ואפילו לקרות ק"ש שרי שהרי איתא במדרש

A very different conclusion is reached by the Taz:

TUREI ZAHAV, ORACH CHAIM 8:

נראה לי שיש איסור גמור מטעם אחר דהיינו כיון שחוק הוא עכשיו בין העכו״ם שעושין כן תמיד תיכף שיושבין פורקין מעליהם הכובע ואם כן זה נכלל בכלל ובחוקותיהם לא תלכו כ״ש בחוק זה שיש טעם דכיסוי הראש מורה על יראת שמים כההיא דסוף שבת כסי רישך כי היכי דליהוי עלך אימתא דמרך

It appears to me that there is a complete prohibition for a different reason. That is, it is an established custom amongst the Gentiles that as soon as they sit down they remove their hat. Therefore, covering one's head becomes a fulfillment of "You shall not follow the practice of the Gentiles." All the more so regarding this practice, as there is good reason for it: covering one's head indicates fear of Heaven. As is seen from the passage in *Masechet Shabbat*, "Cover your head so that you will have fear of Heaven..."

רבה — If not for the fact that I am not accustomed to arguing with the early authorities without the support of a great figure, I would tend to be lenient and permit saying a blessing with a bare head, and even to say the *Shema* is permitted, as the *Midrash* states."

The Taz maintains that our analysis of the earlier sources is moot. The matter of wearing a yarmulke or going bareheaded does not hinge upon the early Talmudic sources. Rather, there is an absolute obligation for all men to wear a yarmulke at all times! His reasoning is as follows: The Torah instructs us not to emulate the Gentiles by following their customs. Prevailing Gentile custom is to remain bareheaded, particularly when showing deference and respect, therefore, Jewish practice must be different and a Jew must wear a hat or yarmulke. According to the Taz, the requirement to wear a yarmulke is a component of the larger demand that Jews set themselves apart from the Gentiles around them. It is therefore an absolute obligation, and failing to wear a yarmulke is a violation of a Torah prohibition.

The Taz provides a sharply different perspective on our discussion. Thus far, we had been looking for an early source in the Talmud, *Midrash*, or at least a medieval Halachic text to provide the basis for the obligation to wear a yarmulke. The Taz tells us that there is no need to search the usual sources, as the requirement to wear a yarmulke is absolute even without an early source. All we need to do is look around at our neighbors. If the Gentile custom is to bare one's head as a sign of respect then we must in turn cover our heads so as not to follow the Gentile practice.[44]

Some explanation is necessary to properly understand the Taz. After all, the Halachah that we must not follow Gentile practices has rules and parameters, like all *Halachot* do. Does the common practice of baring one's head out of respect really qualify as a Gentile custom that we're required to avoid?

It would seem that the answer to this question is no. The Torah restriction against following Gentile practices is intended to keep us away from activities associated with idolatry. Therefore, religious customs are forbidden, as are practices that have no reason at all. In the case of the latter, there is a concern that the custom may have originated in idolatry. However, a Gentile norm that is followed as a sign of respect or the like does not constitute "the custom of the Gentiles" and is not forbidden.[45] Accordingly, if

---

44 This, of course, implies that, conceivably, if the Gentile custom were to change and we'd see them covering their heads, the entire matter would reverse and the Jews would be required to go bareheaded. The Taz does not address this odd potential outcome of his ruling.

45 In *Shulchan Aruch, Yoreh Deah* 178:1: וכל זה אינו אסור אלא בדבר שנהגו בו העובדי כוכבים לשם פריצות כגון שנהגו ללבוש מלבושים אדומים והוא מלבוש שרים וכדומה לזה ממלבושי הפריצות או בדבר שנהגו למנהג ולחוק ואין טעם בדבר דאיכא למיחש ביה משום דרכי האמורי ושיש בו שמץ עבודת כוכבים מאבותיהם אבל דבר שנהגו לתועלת כגון שדרכן שכל מי שהוא רופא מומחה יש לו מלבוש מיוחד שניכר בו שהוא רופא אומן מותר ללובשו וכן שעושין משום כבוד או טעם אחר מותר

the common practice of going bareheaded or baring one's head in the presence of an important person is done as a matter of respect, it would follow that we need not be concerned with disassociating from such a custom. Why would the Taz then rule that we have an absolute obligation to wear a yarmulke based on the requirement to avoid Gentile customs?

A possible explanation is that the custom to bare one's head is in fact not a simple convention of respect. Baring one's head was established by the early Christians as a religious mandate. In his letter to the Corinthians, Paul, one of the early teachers of Christianity, instructs the first Christians that when praying they must bare their heads, as praying or prophesying with a covered head "dishonors the head."[46] If, in fact, uncovering one's head began as a non-Jewish religious practice, it rightfully belongs in the category of Gentile customs we may not follow. Even if subsequently the original religious connotation was lost and it appears to be an innocent sign of respect, going

---

But anything they practice for a reason, for example that it is normal that a doctor wears a unique garment such that he is recognized as a doctor, is permitted to do. Similarly, that which they do for respect or some other reason is permitted.

46 First Book of Corinthians 11:4: "Every man praying or prophesying, having his head covered, dishonors his head."

bareheaded does not lose its association to foreign religious practice. This would certainly be the case in Christian Europe in the times of the Taz, when everyone knew that Christian worship requires a bare head. Even Church notables who would otherwise wear a hat or head covering remove it at times of worship.

Although the Taz does not explicitly state all of the above it would seem reasonable that his categorizing of going bareheaded as a "Gentile custom" is justified based on our explanation.

The Chatam Sofer[47] refers directly to the religious nature of the Gentile custom to go bareheaded. In doing so, he addresses more broadly the significance we associate with wearing a yarmulke. In addition, the Chatam Sofer answers a question we have yet to raise thus far, but a troubling one nonetheless: If, as we saw in the Talmudic passages, the purpose of wearing a head covering is to remind one of G-d's presence and to increase the wearer's fear of heaven, why do we differentiate between men and women? While married women are Biblically obligated to cover their heads for independent reasons, unmarried women and young girls do not wear yarmulkes. Why are they less in need of the benefits of

---

47 R' Moshe Sofer (Germany and Czechoslovakia, 1762–1839), commonly referred to by the name of his work *Chatam Sofer*.

wearing a yarmulke? Let us take a look at the Chatam Sofer's comments:

CHATAM SOFER, COMMENTARY TO *NEDARIM* 30B:

הא דבזמננו מקפידים מאד מאד מבלי לגלות ראש ומחשיב את המגלה לפושע לא נהגו אבותינו כן מטעם מנהג פרישות ויראת שמים דא״כ נשים פנויות נמי דלענין זה אין לחלק... אע״כ לא מטעם חסידות הנהיגו כן אלא מעיקר הדין כמ״ש הט״ז באו״ח סי׳ ח׳ מאחר שעשאוהו עע״ז חק לע״ז לילך דוקא בגלוי ראש ולכבד הע״ז בזה א״כ נאסר לנו מן הדין.... ומנהג זה נהגו בזכרים ולא בנקבות שלהם, אדרבא אית בהו קפידא ביניהם שלא תלכנה בגלוי ראש לבית ע״ז ע״כ לא החמירו אבותינו בגלוי ראש דנקבות פנויות:

In our times we are very strict not to bare our heads, and we consider one who does bare his head to be a transgressor, but our ancestors did not establish this custom for reasons of piety or fear of Heaven. For if that were the reason, unmarried women should do so as well, as in this regard there is no difference... Rather, it must be that they did not begin this practice for piety, but as a basic law, as the Taz writes in *Orach Chaim* 8, that once the Gentiles have established as a religious practice to be bareheaded and to honor their worship thus, the same becomes

> prohibited for us according to the letter of the law... This custom was established for them with respect to males, but not females. On the contrary, they are strict not to allow females in their places of worship bareheaded. Therefore our ancestors were not strict to extend the obligation of head covering to unmarried women.

We learn several important points from the Chatam Sofer:

- **The practice of wearing a yarmulke was established at some point in time.**
  According to the Chatam Sofer there was a conscious decision made at one point to be meticulous about wearing yarmulkes, though he does not identify a time period during which this custom was promulgated. Whether by design or not, this resulted in the attitude that one who does not cover his head is a rebel.

- **The reason for the practice is not rooted in the early sources in the Talmud, *Midrash* and *Zohar*.**

  As noted above, although those sources teach that wearing a yarmulke demonstrates and assists in our awareness of G-d's presence, there are many reasons why the Talmudic and other early sources are inconclusive. Yet, while the Taz simply offers his own reason for the obligation, the Chatam Sofer openly rejects the early sources as the primary reason for the yarmulke. Instead he accepts and strengthens the Taz's explanation that we must conduct ourselves differently than the Gentiles. By noting that the Christians had established as a *rule of their worship* that one must remain bareheaded, the Chatam Sofer justifies the categorization of yarmulke as a fulfillment of "do not follow in their ways."

- **Women are exempt from wearing a yarmulke.**

We know that common practice is that men, and not women, wear yarmulkes. The Torah requires married women to wear a head covering, for reasons associated with the dignity and stature of a married Jewish woman. Unmarried women do not wear yarmulkes or any other head covering, at any time. The Chatam Sofer sees this as proof positive that the requirement to wear a yarmulke does not originate with the passages in the Talmud that praised the yarmulke for its ability to bring a person to fear of Heaven. If the obligation to wear a head covering stemmed from "fear of Heaven," women should not be exempt. If however the requirement to wear a yarmulke is predicated on the Gentile custom, women, who are specifically expected to *not* be bareheaded in places of Gentile worship, were never included in the practice to wear a yarmulke. This actually accords perfectly with the quote above from Paul to the early Christians. In the continuation of his words referenced above, he goes on to instruct that, in contrast to men, women must cover their heads during prayer and that failing to do so is improper.[48] If the custom to wear a yarmulke developed in response to the Gentile practice expressed in the letter to the Corinthians, it makes perfect sense that women were excluded from wearing yarmulkes![49]

---

48 "But every woman who prays or prophesies with her head *uncovered* dishonors her head."

49 In contrast with this analysis is that of R' Ovadia Yosef (Israel, 1920–2013) who ruled that all girls and women must cover their heads while praying and saying blessings, in compliance with the law "one should not mention G-d's name with a bare head" (*Yabia Omer* Vol. 6, *Orach Chaim* 15). This is the contemporary practice among some of R' Yosef's followers,

In summary: we've discovered that according to several later commentators the obligation to wear a head covering does not come from the Talmud. Although no one contests that covering one's head can bring a greater awareness of the Divine Presence, the Taz, Vilna Gaon, and Chatam Sofer all say that this idea does not generate an obligation upon all men. In the eyes of the Vilna Gaon, this leads to the conclusion that there is in fact no general obligation to wear a yarmulke. The Taz and Chatam Sofer, on the other hand, argue that the obligation to wear a yarmulke is absolute and based on the need to set ourselves apart from Gentile customs.

Where does this leave us? In the next chapter we'll see how two later great Halachic codifiers, the authors of *Mishnah Berurah* and *Aruch HaShulchan*, ruled. We'll then turn to the Halachic commentaries of the most recent generations and discover an additional twist to the approaches we've seen thus far.

So I was attending a Jewish summer camp and the boys were expected to wear kippahs. No problem. I like kippahs. Some of the boys wore black. Some blue.

---

but is otherwise a minority view.

Some kippahs had superheroes on them, or sports teams. All fine.

My problem was not the kippah itself. It was getting it to stay on my head, especially during sports.

Some boys used clips. Others used velcro.

I couldn't do either because I didn't have any hair — chemotherapy tends to do that to a person.

Instead, I got a bigger, rounder kippah which perched itself nicely on my head — and had the added benefit of making my baldness a little less obvious (which to a young boy, was quite important). One more reason to love kippahs!

C.M.

CHAPTER 5

In the *Aruch HaShulchan*[50] we find several rulings regarding head coverings. Earlier we mentioned that the *Aruch HaShulchan* explains the concept of covering one's head as a sign of fear of Heaven. He prefaces his own words with quotes from the Talmud in *Kiddushin* regarding R' Huna as well as the story in *Masechet Kallah* involving the child who walked by the Rabbis bareheaded. He then states:

> *ARUCH HASHULCHAN, ORACH CHAIM* 2:10:
>
> והענין שהראש שבו המוח, שהוא מקור החכמה והיראה – אין לו להתגלות לפניו יתברך שמלא כל הארץ כבודו, כמו שאין לעמוד במקום קדוש בגילוי ראש. ואם אינו עושה כן, עזות יצרו מתגבר עליו גם בלא הרגשה.

---

50 Authored by R' Yechiel Michel Halevi Epstein (Belarus, 1829–1908).

והנה יש מן הגדולים הסוברים שמעיקר הדין יש איסור בזה, ויש שסוברים שזהו רק ממידת חסידות. אמנם אם כה ואם כה הנסיון יעיד על זה.

(ובמקום ההכרח, כמו בערכאות הקיר"ה שמדינא דמלכותא אין לילך בכיסוי הראש בשם – מותר. אך שלא במקום הכרח, מי שרוצה לזכות ביראת ה' ישמור את עצמו מזה. ודי למבין.)

The concept is that the head, in which resides the brain, the source of intelligence and fear, should not be bare in the presence of G-d, whose glory fills the entire world. This is similar to the idea of not standing in a holy place while bareheaded. And if one fails to do so, brazenness overcomes him, even if he does not realize.

There are some authorities who ruled that going bareheaded is absolutely forbidden, and others who said that it is an attribute of piety. However, one way or the other, experience can attest to it.

Where one is compelled, such as in the courts of the Tsar, may his glory be elevated, wherein by law of the land one may not go with a covered head, it is permitted. However, where there is no compelling factor — one who wishes to

> achieve fear of Heaven should be careful about this. This is sufficient to one who understands.

In the Aruch HaShulchan's words we see an emphasis on the ability of the yarmulke to bring its wearer to fear of Heaven. Additionally, we see a rationale for the concept: by covering my head, the source of my own greatness as a human being, I demonstrate that there is something greater than myself whose Presence is felt throughout the world.

The Aruch HaShulchan makes reference to those who maintained that wearing a yarmulke is an absolute obligation. Presumably he is referring to the position of the Taz, Chatam Sofer and others who ruled that going bareheaded is a violation of "do not follow the practices of the Gentiles." This is not the opinion the Aruch HaShulchan himself follows, but he does allude to "experience" having demonstrated something. We can only guess what he is referring to, but it is safe to surmise that he felt that whether or not we are actually obligated to wear a yarmulke, doing so is a sign of commitment to G-d while baring one's head demonstrates the opposite. This does echo the words of the Chatam Sofer we read above.

We also read in the *Aruch HaShulchan* that there are circumstances under which removing one's yarmulke would be appropriate. What is most striking in the Aruch HaShulchan's comments is how strongly he advocates wearing a yarmulke, even while acknowledging that there may be no technical requirement to do so.

As we saw above, the need for a head covering during prayer can be independent of the need for a constant yarmulke. What does the Aruch HaShulchan have to tell us about wearing a yarmulke for prayer?

> *ARUCH HASHULCHAN, ORACH CHAIM* 91:
>
> ובמדינתינו אין להתפלל אף כשהראש מכוסה בכיסוי קטן, רק בעינן כובע כמו שהולכין ברחוב... ואסור להוציא אזכרה מפיו בראש מגולה.
>
> In our country, one should not pray if his head is only covered with a small covering, rather one requires a hat in the manner that one walks in the street...
>
> ... It is forbidden to mention G-d's name with a bare head.

There are two distinct issues here. The first line instructs in the proper manner of prayer. One should pray in the clothing he or she usually wears in the street — meaning dignified, "proper" dress. The specific garments may vary from society to society, but the concept remains the same: one should dress for prayer in the same way they would go about respectable business. Therefore, the Aruch HaShulchan's reference to wearing a hat was relevant to his time, but today may not be required, as in our society a hat per se is not a part of the gentleman's attire.

The second sentence in this source is much more definite. The Aruch HaShulchan rules clearly that it is forbidden to say G-d's name with a bare head. This is separate from the need to pray in the manner one walks in the street. The requirement to wear a head covering when saying G-d's name relates back to the idea we saw in the earlier source from the *Aruch HaShulchan*.[51] We express our subservience to G-d by covering our heads, the source of our intelligence. While this is not an absolute requirement as such at all times, it is indeed necessary when actually speaking to or about G-d.

We learned in the *Aruch HaShulchan* three types of potential requirements to don a head covering. Under usual circumstances one is encouraged to wear a yarmulke at all times; when saying G-d's name one must wear a yarmulke (or other head covering); when praying, in addition to covering one's head, one should dress in the dignified dress of that time and place, which could include a hat or anything else for that matter.

---

51 See source on page 82.

We now turn to the Mishnah Berurah[52] for his understanding of, and rulings on, the matter of the yarmulke. Written in the beginning of the nineteenth century, the *Mishnah Berurah* is often viewed as the latest truly authoritative commentator on the first section of *Shulchan Aruch*, *Orach Chaim*, which deals with the laws of the daily routine.

MISHNAH BERURAH, ORACH CHAIM 2:11:

ומידת חסידות אפילו פחות מארבע אמות, ואפילו בעת השינה בלילה. ויש שמצדדין לומר דאפילו ארבע אמות אינו אסור מדינא, רק להצנועין במעשיהן. אבל כבר כתב הט״ז לקמן בסימן ח׳, דבזמנינו איסור גמור מדינא להיות בגילוי הראש, ואפילו יושב בביתו, עיין שם הטעם... ודע עוד, דלעניין גילוי הראש די בכיסוי היד על הראש, והוא הדין אם מפלה ראשו שרי בגילוי הראש...

It is a measure of piety to cover one's head even when walking fewer than four *amot*, and even while asleep at night. There are those who take the position that even walking four *amot* bareheaded is not essentially forbidden, but is

52 *Mishnah Berurah* is a comprehensive commentary on the *Shulchan Aruch*. Its author was R' Yisrael Meir HaKohen Kagan (Lithuania, 1839–1933), who is often refered to by the name of this work or his other famous book, *Chafetz Chaim*.

> for those who are extra meticulous in their actions. However, the Taz already ruled that in our times it is absolutely prohibited to be bareheaded, even while sitting in one's home...
> Know, that for the issue of being bareheaded, it is sufficient to cover one's head with his hand. Also, when one is getting his hair cut, he may be bareheaded.

As noted, the *Mishnah Berurah* is a relatively recent work, and incorporates all the early views on the matter. Though acknowledging the opinion of the Vilna Gaon, that one is not fully obligated to wear a yarmulke, the Mishnah Berurah himself follows the view of the Taz that one must cover his head, ideally at all times, even while sleeping! We recall that the Taz ruled that going bareheaded is a gentile custom and therefore forbidden.

Here we encounter an interesting conclusion. Only under the most impractical of circumstances, when one is getting a haircut, is the Mishnah Berurah willing to give the green light to remove the yarmulke from one's head. On the other hand, because the primary motivation for covering one's head is to separate ourselves from the Gentiles, it may be sufficient to do so by merely using one's hand to cover his head!

This approach, while resulting in a leniency allowing one to cover his head with his hand, also results in a stringency later:

> *MISHNAH BERURAH, ORACH CHAIM* 2:12:
>
> ופרו״ק משערות (פאה נוכרית), אף אותן שתפורין בבגד מתחתיו, יש לאסור מפני מראית העין, שיאמרו ששערות הן. ויש מקילין.
>
> A wig, or toupee, even if connected with material underneath, should be forbidden because of "appearance to the eye," for people will think it is hair. Some are lenient.

The two views cited here regarding a wig correlate directly to the views we've learned thus far. According to the view that a head covering should be worn as a reminder of G-d's presence, any head covering is sufficient. A wig is no different than a hat, a yarmulke, or any other garment. However, if the purpose of the head covering is to demonstratively set us apart from the Gentiles around us, then a wig or toupee, which is meant to look like hair, won't achieve the proper goal.

In the ruling of the Mishnah Berurah we see emphasis on setting ourselves apart from the Gentiles, as expressed in his ruling that ideally one should wear a yarmulke at all times, even when stationary; in his ruling that using one's hand meets the need for a head covering; and in his ruling that a wig is unsatisfactory. It is virtually unnecessary for the Mishnah Berurah to tell us that when praying, saying blessings, and studying Torah we must wear a yarmulke.

Interestingly, the Mishnah Berurah makes particular mention of the need to train young children to wear a yarmulke. This is perfectly consistent with his view that we must visually distinguish ourselves, as well as with the passage from the Talmud above,[53] whereby R' Nachman's mother insisted that he wear a head covering from a young age.[54]

The Mishnah Berurah's view can be contrasted with that of the Aruch HaShulchan we saw above. For the latter, the focus of the yarmulke was to achieve fear of Heaven. Consequently, the Aruch HaShulchan rules that there is no explicit obligation, rather a strong preference to wear a head covering to assist in one's awareness of the Divine Presence. The Aruch HaShulchan seemingly would be entirely satisfied with a wig — at the end of

---

53 See source on p. 12.

54 The Mishnah Berurah bases this ruling on the words of R' Avraham Gombiner (Poland, 1637–1682) in *Magen Avraham*: ובנדרים דף ל"ו משמע דקטנים דרכן לילך בגלוי הראש ועיין ביורה דעה סימן רי"ז סל"ז. ומ"מ נכון לכסות ראשם דתהוי עליהם אימתא דשמיא כדאיתא בסוף שבת עסי' רפ"ב ס"ג והע"ש לא עיין סי' צ"א סק"ו.

the day, the person is wearing something extra on his head, which can assist in fear of Heaven just as much as a yarmulke!

It is possible that the same question raised by the Mishnah Berurah regarding a toupee can be asked nowadays with respect to a baseball cap or the like. Does one fulfill the need for a yarmulke by wearing a baseball cap? If the author of *Aruch HaShulchan* were to be asked, the answer should likely be yes. After all, it is a head covering and can remind the wearer of the Divine Presence. According to the view of the Mishnah Berurah and those whom he followed, one could argue that a baseball cap does nothing to set us apart from the Gentiles around us and would therefore not address the requirement for a yarmulke.

I'm forty years old. I have a job, a house, a car, a mortgage, and a great wife and kids. I'm supposed to be a grown-up and comfortable in my own skin.

So why does wearing a kippah send me into philosophical quandaries?

Don't get me wrong. I'm an observant Jew and I try to keep my head covered.

Unless I'm at work (why bring religion into the workplace?).

Or on the subway (never know when some unpleasant anti-Semitic something will happen, why look for trouble?)

Or exercising.

I guess I don't end up wearing one as often as I'd like.

N. C.

CHAPTER 6

In more recent years, the various ideas and disparate strands we've learned have become interwoven. Taken together, they form a new obligation to wear a yarmulke which, for us, may be the strongest reason yet.

We've seen a selection of the literature on the topic of wearing a head covering, with views ranging from those who mandate a yarmulke at all times to those who don't even technically require a head covering for prayer. However, it seems clear that for many centuries the common practice of observant, G-d fearing Jews was to wear a yarmulke. It is likely that this custom began with the early sources we saw, advocating a head covering to assist in fear of Heaven and praising those who wore one. Although perhaps not an obligation, wouldn't we *want* to remind ourselves of G-d's constant presence? Later on, as Christian practice became dominant, the idea developed that we also cover our heads to show we differ from those surrounding us. What resulted is the widely observed and acknowledged practice to wear a yarmulke as the mark of a devout Jew. Conversely, removing one's yarmulke became an act of rebellion and defiance against the G-d of Israel.

This source of obligation, though nebulous at times, is the binding nature of *Minhag Yisrael*, the accepted practice of the observant community. Often the potency of *minhag* is so strong that it can outlast, and sometimes even preserve, laws that would appear to have more authoritative origins. Such is the power of this particular custom that although we are scattered across the globe, the sight of another person with a yarmulke across the street in an unfamiliar place immediately identifies that person as my brother, to whom I'll gravitate if I need assistance or maybe just share a nod and a smile.

This idea, or slight variations thereof, was expressed by R' Ovadia Yosef[55] and R' Shlomo Zalman Auerbach,[56] both towering Torah giants and leaders of recent decades. Both

---

55 Iraq; Israel, 1920–2013. Was considered the foremost leader of Sephardic Jews for two generations.

56 Israel, 1910-1995. Was one of the most highly regarded and influential Halachic authorities of the 20th century.

ruled that it is imperative, even under difficult circumstances, to wear a yarmulke as a sign of one's association to a community of G-d fearing Jews.

In this vein, the yarmulke is not merely an article of clothing. It is part of a uniform and a banner declaring that one is mindful of his Maker. But it's not sufficient to proclaim this outwardly. Ultimately, as we saw above, the goal is for this awareness to permeate through the wearer's consciousness. My realization of G-d's presence is supposed to inform my values, my choices, my actions and my thoughts. The success of this endeavor is all the more powerful when it is shared in a public and obvious way along with a larger group of like-minded individuals.

The ultimate goal of the yarmulke is demonstrated in the following story, unfortunate as it may be.

> Gil Fried, an Orthodox Jew and a sports law professor at the University of Houston, had donned his basic black yarmulke for three years without incident in California courts. But, on September 4, 1996, when he appeared in the courtroom of Houston state court Judge Patricia Lykos, Fried hit a snag. He was scheduled to testify as an expert witness on behalf of a plaintiff suing a roller skate manufacturer

in a personal injury matter. Just minutes before, while conferring in court with the plaintiff's attorney, Fried was called into Lykos' chambers. That is when she ordered Fried to remove his yarmulke or be barred from testifying in her courtroom.

Fried was shocked and bewildered. He told Judge Lykos that in all of his years as a litigator in California he had never before been asked to remove his yarmulke. Fried tried to impress upon her the religious significance for him in wearing the yarmulke. Judge Lykos responded that wearing the yarmulke might prejudice the jury into thinking that Fried had religious authority, and that since it was her court, if he wanted to testify, he had to take it off. [57]

Judge Lykos was concerned that the jurors, seeing a yarmulke, would assume that its wearer automatically was a more reliable and trustworthy witness, bearing "religious authority."

Though Judge Lykos was wrong in her insistence that Mr. Fried remove his yarmulke, and her actions violated

---

57 http://www.nytimes.com/1996/10/06/us/witness-files-complaint-as-yarmulke-is-banned-by-texas-court.html

Mr. Fried's constitutional rights, this story highlights the potential of the yarmulke. My yarmulke should rightfully attest to my upright character and high moral standards, to the point that even an outsider will identify me as representing those attributes. Most importantly, if I simply wear the yarmulke while failing to live up to these standards, the purpose of the yarmulke has eluded me.

This courtroom disagreement brings us to our next question. Is it ever, and under what circumstances may it be, appropriate to remove one's yarmulke and go bareheaded? Should Mr. Fried have complied with Judge Lykos? Let us continue.

I'll tell you something interesting. I've never worn a kippah in public or at home. Only in synagogue for the occasional wedding or Jewish affair. But when I got off the plane in Israel for the first time, somehow a kippah found its way to my head. I hadn't even consciously packed it in my carry-on bag. I thought of bringing it to go to the Western Wall but somehow my heart knew to have it closer at hand.

True, the majority of Israelis don't consider themselves "religious," though I think they believe far more than they realize.

After all, why replant yourselves in our ancient home and put up with terrorism and economic boycotts if deep down you don't think this is all really, really important and — at a certain level — true?

So even though much of Israel is a modern secular country, deep down I feel it is a very religious place. Heck, this is where Abraham and Sarah walked. This is where King David fought the Philistines and wrote the Psalms. This is where Rabbi Akiva was tortured to death and in his final words said the Shema... this isn't just any land. This is the one and only Jewish homeland.

I don't look like a particular religious person on the outside, and I don't often act in the most Jewish way — but this is Israel, and I'm a Jew. And when I walk around this land, I do so with a kippah on my head.

H.K.

CHAPTER 7

Let's assume you've been convinced by reading the previous chapters that wearing a yarmulke is a really important thing to do, perhaps even a requirement. In fact, it's a relatively easy way to identify with other Jews all over the world and to proudly proclaim the values one holds dear.

But it's not always so simple to wear a yarmulke, or even a cap. For some, it may be a general discomfort with being conspicuous. Well, that's part of the point. The yarmulke is supposed to be obvious. However, beyond the general discomfort, which one can choose to overcome, there are circumstances under which one is instructed or expected not to wear a head covering. How should one react?

In the story above, a judge insisted that a witness in her court remove his yarmulke. This was not the first time such an event occurred. We have records in rabbinic literature of similar incidents taking place hundreds of years ago, and as a result we have rabbinic input on this question as well.

Our first source deals with more extreme conditions than a judge in a Texas courtroom. The following question was raised in the 15th century by R' Yisrael Isserlein.[58] If one is passing through a region where Jews are targeted for kidnapping, is he allowed to dress as a Gentile, which would entail walking bareheaded and wearing a garment made of wool and linen combined, and thereby avoid recognition?[59]

TERUMAT HADESHEN, RESPONSA 196:

משמע דאסור להתדמות לנכרי כדי שלא יכירוהו, ולאו דווקא ללבוש כלאים אלא אפי׳...ללכת בכל העיר בגילוי הראש, כל אילו הצורות סוברים הנכרים באשכנז שהוא אסור גמור לבר ישראל כמו כלאים בבגדים, והעושה אותו

---

58 R' Yisrael Isserlein (Austria, 1390-1460) composed *Terumat Hadeshen* as a work of Halachic Responsa, though there is some discussion as to whether the questions posed were actual queries addressed to R' Isserlein or theoretical situations contrived by the author.

59 This is the Biblical prohibition known as *shaatnez*, based on the verse in *Devarim* 22:11: לֹא תִלְבַּשׁ שַׁעַטְנֵז צֶמֶר וּפִשְׁתִּים יַחְדָּו. Do not wear *shaatnez* – wool and linen mixed together.

נראה ככופר... אמנם י״ל דדוקא כדי להבריח המכס אסור, אבל בשביל סכנה כההיא דס׳ חסידים, וכמו שאלותינו שרי.. אמנם בנ״ד כדמבואר בשאלתינו צ״ע אי חשיב סכנה, הואיל ומתחילה מכניס א״ע לכך לעבור דרך אותו מדינה, ולא דמי לעובדא דרבי מאיר ולההוא דס׳ חסידים שבא הסכנה עליו שלא ברצונו... ולכך צריך לדקדק יפה בדברים הללו שלא יהא נראה כמודה בע״ז, שכל המודה בה כאלו כופר בכל התורה כולה, הנראה לע״ד כתבתי.

We learn that it is forbidden to pose as a Gentile so that he will not be recognized. This is not limited to wearing a garment made of wool and linen, rather even... to walk in the city with a bare head. All of these are assumed by the Gentiles in *Ashkenaz*[60] to be completely forbidden to a Jew, and one who does so appears to be a heretic... However it is possible that doing so is forbidden only when avoiding an excessive tax, but when there is actual danger, as in our question, it may be permitted. But even in our case, one must analyze whether in fact this is actual danger, as the person chose to pass through that area, where it was known that this danger

60 In medieval rabbinic literature, Ashkenaz refers to a region comprised of parts of modern Germany, Austria and northern France.

> would be encountered. Such is different than circumstances where the danger came upon him unwillingly... Therefore one must be extremely cautious in these matters, so as not to appear to accept idolatry. For one who acknowledges idolatry rejects the entire Torah.

Unfortunately, throughout Jewish history there have been times when Jews were motivated to hide their Jewish identity. Doing so however can be highly problematic due to the potential indication that one subscribes to a different faith. The latter of course is a very grave matter, and could even be forbidden in a situation of actual danger. Although we are not usually faced with life threatening circumstances as a result of our yarmulkes, the words of the *Terumat Hadeshen* are illuminating for several reasons.

- **It was accepted and common practice for Jews of this period to wear a head covering.** First and foremost, the premise of the question is that a Jew wears a yarmulke and going bareheaded will assist him in posing as a non-Jew. At the very least, we learn here that in the mid-fifteenth century head coverings were worn by all Ashkenazic Jews.

- **There is no inherent prohibition to go bareheaded.**

  The reservations expressed in *Terumat Hadeshen* derive from the concern that one may appear to accept idolatry. Going bareheaded is not treated as an independent source of concern. Thus, while on the one hand it is clear that all Jews did wear a head covering of some sort, it is likewise evident that failing to do so was not seen as a particular violation of a law as such.

- **Deliberately hiding one's Jewish identity is generally forbidden.**

  The very nature of the question, as well as the hesitancy of the author to permit changes to one's attire, highlight the severity of denying one's Jewishness. Deliberately hiding one's Jewishness by dressing as a Gentile comes very close to actively denying that one is Jewish. The author of *Terumat Hadeshen* permits doing so only when the individual is thrust into an involuntary situation of actual danger. This is the final and authoritative ruling of the *Shulchan Aruch* as well.[61]

---

61 *Yoreh Deah* 157.

We live in times and under circumstances very different than those described in the *Terumat Hadeshen*, thus this ruling cannot be directly applied to modern times for a host of reasons. His comments are nonetheless important, for they establish the three points we highlighted and serve as an important backdrop to any discussion of removing one's yarmulke.

Luckily, the very same author addressed a somewhat more familiar variation of our question. Is one permitted to take an oath in a non-Jewish court while bareheaded?

> *TERUMAT HADESHEN, PSAKIM* 103:
>
> ואשר כתבת על ההוא גזירה שחדשו השלטונים בבריסלא"ו, שהיהודים המחוייבים שבועה יצטרכו לישבע בשם המיוחד בקריאתו להדיא ובגילוי הראש, וס"ל לדמות זה לשמדא דשנוי ערקתא דמסנא... ובגלוי הראש לא אשכחן קפידא להדיא לאיסור
>
> As to what you wrote regarding the decree recently passed by the authorities in Breslau, that Jews who are obligated to take an oath will be forced to do so using G-d's name as it is explicitly read and while bareheaded: You wished to compare this situation to one of forced apostasy... We don't find a clear prohibition against being bareheaded.

Note that the author of *Terumat Hadeshen* is not discussing whether or not one should wear a yarmulke on a regular basis. It was clear to him that this was the universal Jewish practice in his area. He does however acknowledge that when push comes to shove, and there are circumstances whereby a Jew must remove his yarmulke, doing so is not an inherent sin.[62] As we saw in his earlier remarks, removing the yarmulke to hide one's Jewishness is a distinct issue that does not speak directly to the matter of going bareheaded.

We now fast-forward several centuries in our exploration of this topic. R' David Tzvi Hoffmann,[63] in late nineteenth century Germany, was also asked whether one is permitted to take an oath in a non-Jewish court with a bare head. In his response we discover several points of interest.

> *MELAMED L'HO'IL* VOL. 2 CH. 56:
> ועיין גם בבית הלל לי״ד סי׳ קנ״ז דהיו נותנים שוחד שלא יצטרכו לישבע בגילוי ראש. והנה בעת הזאת הרבנים היראים במדינות אונגארן מחמירין מאד בענין גלוי ראש...

62 In the specific case he was addressing, the larger issue was mentioning G-d's name explicitly. Note that even though the individual would in fact be saying G-d's name, the author permits doing so while bareheaded under the circumstances.

63 Germany, 1843–1921.

הנה בק״ק יראים דפפד״מ בבית החינוך שנתיסד מהגאון ר׳ שמשון רפאל הירש זצ״ל (שאני הייתי מורה שם ב׳ שנים וחצי) יושבים התלמידים בשעת לימוד שאר המדעים בפריעת ראש, ורק בשעת לימוד תורה מכסים ראשם (וכן הוא המנהג בבית הספר בהאמבורג) וזה נעשה שם עפ״י תקנת הרה״ג מו״ה ש״ר הירש זצ״ל.

ובפעם ראשון שבאתי לביתו של הרה״ג ש״ר הירש בכובע על ראשי, אמר לי שכאן הוא דרך ארץ להסיר הכובע מעל הראש כשבאין אל אדם חשוב, ואולי יראה מורה אחר (יש בבית החינוך שם גם הרבה מורים א״י) שאני איני מסיר הכובע מעל הראש לפני ראש בית החינוך (דירעקטאר) היה מחשב זה כאילו אני מבזה אותו. ובזה וכיוצא בזה אין בו משום בחוקותיהם.

ואם כן בנידון דידן אם השופט נותן רשות לכסות הראש בשעת השבועה מה טוב, וכל אחד בודאי לכתחלה צריך לבקש מהשופט לכסות ראשו ויאמר כי הוא מצווה לכסות ראשו בכל דבר שבקדושה והשבועה הוא לו בלתי ספק דבר קדושה. אמנם אם השופט אינו רוצה לתת לו רשות א״צ לקבל עליו אפי׳ עונש ממון ויכול לישבע אפילו בגילוי ראש...

See the work *Beit Hillel* on *Yoreh Deah*, where it is noted that they would pay a bribe to avoid taking oaths with a bare head. Nowadays the Rabbis in the Hungarian areas are very strict about not going bareheaded...

In the holy community of Frankfurt de Main, in the school that was established by the great R' Samson Raphael Hirsch, where I taught for two-and-a-half years, the students sit during the study of sciences with bare heads. Only while studying Torah do they cover their heads (this is also done in the school in Hamburg) and this was instituted by our great Master and Teacher R' S.R. Hirsch...

The first time that I came to the home of R' S.R. Hirsch wearing my hat, he informed me that in this place it is polite to remove one's hat when visiting a distinguished person and that if a non-Jewish teacher at the school would see that I do not remove my hat in the presence of the Director he may think that I am being disrespectful. In such a case there is no issue of "do not follow Gentile customs."

Therefore, in our case if the judge gives permission for the individual to cover his head while taking an oath that would be good. Everyone should ask the judge in the first place for permission and state that he is commanded to cover his head for holy matters — taking an oath being an example of a holy matter. However, if the judge

> refuses to grant permission, he need not sustain even a monetary penalty and is permitted to take the oath with a bare head.

R' Hoffmann prefaces his own nuanced approach with an acknowledgment that there were many authorities who were quite strict on the matter of the yarmulke. Perhaps the most instructive element in this source is the range of views we find regarding the general severity of going bareheaded. On the one extreme we have those who would pay a bribe to avoid swearing in court without a yarmulke, while on the other hand we read about R' Hirsch who, following the norms of his time and place, guided his community not to wear yarmulkes when doing so would be viewed as improper.

And yet R' Hoffmann himself does not fully embrace the lenient position. After relating his personal experience with R' Hirsch and the custom of the Frankfurt community, he rules that one who must take an oath in court should ideally attempt to keep his yarmulke on. Only if the judge refuses to allow the yarmulke should the person remove his head covering and avoid any possible fine or punishment. With this statement R' Hoffmann reminds us that wearing a yarmulke is not a commandment, nor is going bareheaded an actual prohibition. In either of the latter cases, one would indeed be obligated to spend money to fulfill a *mitzvah* or avoid a sin!

We already saw these words of the *Aruch HaShulchan*, reflecting a similar position:

> *ARUCH HASHULCHAN, ORACH CHAIM* 2:
>
> ובמקום ההכרח, כמו בערכאות הקיר״ה שמדינא דמלכותא אין לילך בכיסוי הראש בשם – מותר. אך שלא במקום הכרח, מי שרוצה לזכות ביראת ה׳ ישמור את עצמו מזה. ודי למבין
>
> Where one is compelled, such as in the courts of the Tsar, may his glory be elevated, wherein by law of the land one may not go with a covered head, it is permitted. However, where there is no compelling factor; one who wishes to achieve fear of Heaven should be careful about this. This is sufficient to one who understands.

This ruling is straightforward: If one is in a place where by law it is forbidden to wear a yarmulke, there is no issue with removing it. Nevertheless, the author reminds us that at all other times wearing a yarmulke is strongly advised.

Let us summarize what we've seen thus far regarding removing one's yarmulke. As noted, everything we've read in this chapter presupposes that a yarmulke is generally worn by all Jewish men. We read that there were those who went to great lengths to avoid ever being in a position where they would be compelled to remove their yarmulke. We then saw the view that such efforts are unnecessary and one may take the oath in court bareheaded. Taking it a small step further is the view that one may go bareheaded in any place where the law requires it.[64] Finally, we learned of the custom of the Frankfurt community, instituted by R' Samson Raphael Hirsch, that in any setting where a polite person would remove his hat it was deemed appropriate to do so.

Perhaps unsurprisingly, the various customs today follow a similar spectrum. Practices range from those who will turn heaven and earth to wear a yarmulke even when against protocol, such as our story with Mr. Fried and many like-minded individuals, all the way to those who wear a yarmulke while praying, studying or the like, but would never go about their daily business with a yarmulke.

---

64 Although there is a general concept in Halachah that one must follow the "law of the land", this is limited to areas related to taxation and financial transactions. If a local law would forbid wearing *tefillin* or keeping Kosher, this rule would not apply. Hence, the reason to remove one's yarmulke in the court is not because local law trumps Halachah, but rather because the Halachah itself here is lenient regarding the yarmulke.

Let us see one final source which, while acknowledging the existence of leniencies, strongly supports wearing a yarmulke at all times. R' Moshe Feinstein[65] was one of the foremost Halachic authorities of the twentieth century, particularly in the United States, where a new genre of Halachic query was arising as the American Jewish community flourished. He was asked whether one may take a job where employees are required to go bareheaded.

IGROT MOSHE, CHOSHEN MISHPAT 1:93

ובדבר אם מותר לקבל עבודה במקום שיצטרך ללכת בגילוי ראש, פשוט שמותר דאינו מחוייב להפסיד ממון בשביל זה דאינו איסור ממש אף מדרבנן אלא הוא מנהג טוב, שודאי לא חמור מבטול עשה שאינו מחוייב להפסיד סך גדול, ומניעה מליקח עבודה שהיא עיקר פרנסתו הוא כהפסד גדול[66]...

---

65 Lithuania, New York, 1895-1986.

66 Here Rabbi Feinstein addresses the view that there is in fact an actual prohibition:

ואף להט"ז שסובר שבזה"ז הוא אסור מצד חק עכו"ם שא"כ הוא לאו שיש לאסור אף במקום הפסד ממון, הא לבד שאין דינו ברור הנה תלוי דבר זה להט"ז בהמקומות ובמדינה זו ודאי אין זה משום חק עכו"ם דרובן אינם זהירים בחוקיהם.

This is true even according to the Taz, who maintains that there is a prohibition [to go bareheaded] due to it being a Gentile practice, and in which case it is a Torah prohibition, for which one is obligated to sustain a loss. In addition to the fact that his ruling is not clear, such a matter will depend on the time and place; and here in this country this is not a matter

> אבל ודאי רק במקום עבודתו שע״ז הם מקפידין יהיה רשאי
> אבל כשיצא לחדר אחר וכ״ש כשיצא לשוק יהיה אסור אף
> אם ילעיגו עליו כיון שלא יפסיד משרתו ועבודתו בשביל זה.
>
> Regarding the matter of taking a job in a place where one must go bareheaded: clearly it is permitted, for one is not obligated to lose money over it, being as walking bareheaded is not a prohibition per se, even rabbinically. Rather, it is a good custom, which is certainly no more severe than a positive *mitzvah* for which one is not obligated to lose a large sum. Refraining from taking a job, which is one's source of livelihood is akin to losing a large sum.[67]
>
> But certainly he is only allowed to go bareheaded at the place of his work, but when he goes to a different room, and certainly when he goes out to the street he must wear a head covering, even if he will be ridiculed, so long as he won't lose his job over it.

On the one hand R' Feinstein takes a straightforward lenient approach: there is no clear prohibition to go bareheaded, hence one may take a job at a location where he

---

of idolatrous practice, as most people are not careful about such practices.

67 See previous note.

will not be able to wear a yarmulke. On the other hand, R' Feinstein sees the practice of wearing a yarmulke as largely obligatory, to the extent that one must wear a yarmulke even if he will suffer ridicule as a result. Only the prospect of losing one's livelihood is a sufficient reason for leniency.

Rulings such as R' Feinstein's were heavily relied upon as Jews integrated into general society in the United States during the twentieth century. For many, removing the yarmulke for work has come to be standard practice, even if there is no compelling reason to do so. Based on what we've seen, minor discomfort at being conspicuous is not considered justification to go bareheaded. On the contrary, the very purpose of the yarmulke is to serve as a constant reminder of G-d's presence and the elevated standards by which we're expected to live.

The complex nature of the leniency to go bareheaded for work is demonstrated in this anecdote.

> At the end of his second year in law school, Baruch Cohen was invited to interview for a job with a Wall Street law firm. This was a total surprise, as he had not applied for a position with the "white shoe" firm, which normally courted straight-A, Ivy League WASP-y

students. Baruch, in contrast, attended a mid-level law school, was obviously Jewish, and didn't have a perfect GPA. The dean told him, "I have no idea why you got this opportunity but I suggest you not wear your yarmulke to the interview. And make sure those white strings aren't coming out of your belt."

Coming from a long line of Orthodox rabbis and committed to his Judaism, Baruch was torn. "I grew up in a tough Far Rockaway neighborhood," he recalls. "Where I come from, anyone telling me to take off my kippah was usually angling for a fight." He asked advice from rabbis and orthodox attorneys he knew: wear the kippah for the interview or not? Everyone advised he remove it for this potentially career-making opportunity.

With his kippah in his pocket, Baruch walked into the interview feeling almost as if he were shirtless. He was stunned to see that the attorney sitting there wore a huge velvet yarmulke and *tzitzit*. His first question to Baruch was, "Where's your yarmulke?"

Too shocked to speak, Baruch learned that this attorney had seen him clerking in court, noticed his kippah and decided to offer him an interview. As the young law student stood there defenseless, the elder man laced into him. "You're a sellout," he said. "This is a firm of leaders, not followers." The interview ended before it began.[68]

When I was five or six, I went to a day camp run by the local JCC (Jewish Community Center) near my home in Buffalo, NY. While everyone at the camp was Jewish, I was the only camper who was observant — and the only kid wearing a yarmulke. My counselor, I can't remember her name, kindly told me on the first day that I had forgotten to remove it from my head. I responded that I wore it all day.

She was surprised.

"Doesn't that make you feel self-conscious?" she asked.

"Yes!" I responded with great conviction. "That's why I wear it!"

She was even more surprised.

68 J. Gruen, Attorney For Israel (2013) *Aish.com*, retrieved from http://www.aish.com/jw/s/Attorney-for-Israel.html and reproduced with the author's permission.

And impressed. You can only imagine the smile on my mother's face when the counselor called her that evening to say how smart I was, how I was a proud Jew, how even at my tender age I understood that a yarmulke is supposed to remind us of G-d and keep us in line....

Actually, I had just responded randomly — at five years old, I had no idea what self-conscious meant!

Rabbi Yaacov Haber

CONCLUSION

What should we conclude from our exploration of the rabbinic and historical sources on the matter of the yarmulke?

Hopefully, we've learned that wearing a yarmulke is an intriguing obligation. It is certainly very different than "classical *mitzvot*" such as eating matzah on Passover or lighting candles on Chanuka. In those instances, each obligation, as well as the detailed parameters of the given requirement, is set forth either in the Torah itself or in the Talmud and its commentaries. The yarmulke is not comparable to these *mitzvot*. Nowhere in the Torah or the Talmud do we find a requirement to wear a yarmulke.

Yet wearing a yarmulke is an identifying mark of the Jew and has been so for many centuries. It can be a burden, a part of the uniform, or a badge of honor. It is up to us as individuals to choose how to wear our yarmulkes. What remains clear, however, from the source material and from empirical observation, is that a Jewish man who wishes to identify himself as a member of the community wears a yarmulke. While there are traditions that permit its removal on specific occasions, the yarmulke is a necessary part of the Jew's attire. Thus we remain cognizant not only of G-d's constant presence, but of our own unique mission as a people.

Finally, what of R' Pinchas Shapiro, the protagonist of our opening anecdote? Why did he refuse to walk without a yarmulke, even at pain of extra blows and perhaps danger to his life? Perhaps for R' Pinchas this was a spiritual moment, during which he was beaten for being Jewish and withstanding the blows was a sanctification of G-d's name. A major component of Chassidic teaching is to use each and every activity and experience as a means to sancitfy Hashem's name. As a Chassidic Jew, R' Pinchas's ordeal may have been for him akin to prayer or Torah study, and like the latter instances, an activity absolutely requiring a yarmulke.

GLOSSARY

Aggadah/Aggadic: the sections of the Talmud and other rabbinic literature that teach values, morals, and ethics, as opposed to the Halachic sections that set forth the rules and parameters of ritual obligations. Aggadic teachings are often presented in the context of stories, metaphors and allegories. See Halachah and *Midrash* below.

amot: plural of *amah*, a Talmudic unit of linear measurement known as a "cubit." A cubit is measured as the distance between an average person's elbow and middle finger. Opinions regarding the exact length of the *amah* range from 17.7" to 23".

Arba'ah Turim: lit. "Four Pillars," is the name of the early code of Jewish law authored by R' Yaakov ben Asher (1269-c.1343) in the 14th century. This work was the predecessor to R' Yosef Karo's *Shulchan Aruch*. The "Four Pillars" refer to the four main sections of the work: *Orach Chaim*, laws governing daily activity, including prayers, blessings, Shabbat and holidays; *Yoreh Deah*, ritual laws including Kosher, circumcision; *Even Ha'Ezer,* laws regarding marriage and divorce; and *Choshen Mishpat,* which deals with all financial interactions between Jews.

Ashkenaz/Ashkenazi: Ashkenaz is the name used in medieval rabbinic literature for the Germany/Austria area, mostly the Rhineland. In later years it came to refer collectively to the Jewish communities of Northern Europe, including Hungary, Poland and Russia. An Ashkenazi is a Jew whose family traces its roots to one of these communities. In contrast, Sephardi refers to a Jew whose family originates from the Iberian Peninsula, North Africa or the Middle East.

Baalei HaTosafot: often referred to as the Tosafists. These were the German and French Rabbis of the 12th and 13th centuries whose academies produced glosses on the Talmud (see below) known as the *Tosafot* (lit. additions). The teachings and traditions of the *Baalei HaTosafot* form the basis for the Ashkenazic community's practices.

Bamidbar: the Book of Numbers, the fourth of the Five Books of the Torah.

Beit Yosef: commentary of R' Yosef Karo (1488-1575) to the *Arba'ah Turim* (see above). R' Karo is often referred to as the Beit Yosef, as he is in this work.

Beraitah: teachings of the Oral Law that were not ultimately included in the Mishnah when the latter was formally canonized. See Mishnah below.

Birkat Hamazon: lit. "The blessing of the food," often referred to as the Grace After Meals. It is a four-part blessing required after any meal at which bread is eaten.

brachah (pl-brachot): blessing.

Choshen Mishpat: see above *Arba'ah Turim*.

Darkei Moshe: commentary on *Arba'ah Turim* (see above) by R' Moshe Isserles (1520-1572) of Cracow, Poland. This work supplements the *Arba'ah Turim* and *Beit Yosef* by adding the views and rulings followed in the Ashkenazic communities, where these differ from the rulings of the *Arba'ah Turim* and *Beit Yosef*.

Devarim: the Book of Deuteronomy, fifth of the Five Books of the Torah.

Even Ha'ezer: see above, *Arba'ah Turim*.

gerah: a Biblical measure of weight and currency.

Halachah/Halachic: lit. "walking," refers to the parameters for proper fulfillment of the Torah's requirements in real life. Halachah sets forth the rules that govern a Jew's conduct and fulfillment of the *mitzvot* (Commandments).

Kallah Rabbati: lit. "the Great Bride," a *Beraitah* - section of the Oral Law that was not included in the Mishnah, dealing with some laws and customs of marriage and family life. See *Beraitah* above and Mishnah below.

Masechet Kiddushin: a tractate of the Talmud that deals with some of the laws of marriage. See Mishnah and Talmud below.

kippah: one of the names used for the small cap worn by Jews as a head covering.

Kohen (pl–Kohanim): refers to the descendants of Aharon, Moshe's (Moses) brother; they ultimately became the priests who served in the Temple in Jerusalem. In post-Temple times, when no actual service (e.g. sacrifices) is done, they retain their status as Priests and are responsible for certain functions, including the redemption of the firstborn sons of non-Kohanim. See *pidyon haben* below.

Kol Bo: one of the works of R' Aharon HaKohen of Narbonne, France (13th-14th centuries). This work is a summary of the laws and customs the author learned from his teachers.

mamzer: a child born out of a sexual liaison that is forbidden according to the Torah.

Masechet Avodah Zara: a tractate of the Talmud that deals with the laws of idolatry and idol worship.

Masechet Kallah: lit. "Tractate of the Bride," a parallel *Beraitah* to *Kallah Rabbati*. See entries, *Beraitah*; *Kallah Rabbati*; Mishnah.

Masechet Soferim: lit. "Tractate of Scribes," a *Beraitah* detailing some of the laws of Torah scrolls, *tefillin, mezuzah*, and other ritual laws, including some laws of prayer. See *Beraitah* and *Mishnah*.

Masechet Megillah: lit. "Tractate of the Megillah," this is the portion of the Mishnah and Talmud that details the laws of Purim. Included in those laws is the topic of the Book of Esther, which leads to a broader discussion of the reading of the Holy Scriptures.

Midrash: texts written in the first two centuries of the common era connecting the teachings of the Oral Law to their sources in the Written Law (Five Books of Moses). These teachings can be technical in nature, defining the laws of the Torah, or conveying the morals, values, and ethics of the Torah via interpretation of the texts in the Torah. These two genres are identified as "Midrash Halachah" and "Midrash Aggadah," respectively. See *Aggadah* and Halachah above.

Migbaot: the hats prescribed by the Torah for the *Kohanim* when they served in the Temple. See *Kohanim* above.

Minhag Yisrael: lit. "custom of Israel," referring to the accepted practice of the Jewish community.

Mishnah: the first of the books of the Oral Law (*Torah SheBa'al Peh*). The teachings of the Oral Law were transmitted from teacher to student from the Revelation at Sinai until the Second Temple period, when the Rabbis deemed it necessary to commit these teachings to writing. After a lengthy process of redaction, the Mishnah emerged as the foundational book of the Oral Law's teachings. Both the Babylonian and Jerusalem Talmuds are structured as commentary to the Mishnah, though they go well beyond interpreting the Mishnah alone (see Talmud below).

mitzvah (pl-mitzvot): the Commandments of the Torah.

niddah: a menstruating woman. According to Torah law, a menstruating woman is forbidden to be intimate with her husband and must immerse in a *mikveh* (ritual bath) after her period prior to being with her husband.

Orach Chaim: See *Arba'ah Turim* and *Shulchan Aruch*.

pidyon haben: the Torah obligation to redeem every firstborn male child once the child reaches 30 days of age. The *Kohen* acts as a "representative" of G-d and receives the redemption money from the parents of the child.

poche'ach: one whose appearance is not acceptable. The precise definition and resulting laws are discussed at length in our text.

Rambam: common reference to Maimonides or R' Moshe ben Maimon (1135-1204).

Rif: acronym of ר' יצחק אלפסי, referring to R' Yitzchak Alfasi (1013-1103), a leader of North African Jewry. He was one of the earliest and most authoritative Halachic codifiers in the Sephardic community.

Rishonim: lit. "the early ones," refers to the Torah scholars and authors of the Middle Ages, usually of the 10th to 15th centuries.

Rosh: acronym for רבינו אשר, referring to Rabbenu Asher (c.1250-1327), a student of the German Tosafists who later became a leading rabbinic figure in Spain.

selah/selaim: an ancient measure of weight and currency, found numerous times in the Talmud.

Shabbat: the Torah's Sabbath, observed on Saturday.

shaliach tzibbur: lit. "the agent of the community," refers to the cantor or leader of the communal prayer service.

shaatnez: forbidden mixture of wool and linen in one garment, as prohibited by the Torah.

Shechinah: the Divine Presence.

Shema: the affirmation of G-d's unity recited by Jews each morning and evening.

Shemot: Exodus, the second of the Five Books of the Torah.

Shulchan Aruch: lit. "The Set Table," this is the authoritative code of Jewish law compiled by R' Yosef Karo, with additions by R' Moshe Isserles, in the 16th century (see *Arba'ah Turim*, *Beit Yosef*, and *Darkei Moshe* above). The *Shulchan Aruch* follows the same four-part structure and further subdivision as the *Arba'ah Turim* (outlined above).

speisrutten: a punishment administered by the military court under the Russian Tsar. Described in detail in the text.

tallit: four-cornered prayer shawl fringed with the *tzitzit* (see below) at each corner.

talmid chacham: a Torah scholar.

Talmud: encyclopedic collection of the teachings of the Oral Law, structured as a commentary on the Mishnah (see above), canonized around the 6th century of the Common Era. The Talmud was produced by the academy of the Diaspora in Babylonia; this is known as the Babylonian Talmud or *Talmud Bavli,* as well as by the smaller academy in the Land of Israel. The latter is known as the Jerusalem Talmud or *Talmud Yerushalmi*. The Babylonian Talmud is viewed as the more authoritative text, and, as such, represents the foundation for normative Halachic practice.

Tannaim: the Torah scholars and teachers of the early centuries of the Common Era. They were the authors or contributors to the Mishnah, *Beraitah*, and the various forms of *Midrash* (see above).

tefillin: commonly translated as "phylacteries," the Torah requires each Jewish male to don these boxes daily as a sign and affirmation of our commitment to G-d and His Torah.

Terumat Hadeshen: work of Halachic Responsa written by R' Yisrael Isserlein (Austria, 1390-1460).

Tosafists: English for *Baalei HaTosafot* (See above).

tzitzit: the fringes required by the Torah on four-cornered garments worn by men. Usually used to refer to the garment worn by many Jews to deliberately fulfill this *mitzvah*.

Tur: abbreviated reference to *Arba'ah Turim* (see above).

Yoreh Deah: See above *Arba'ah Turim* and *Shulchan Aruch*.

Zohar: ancient foundational work of Jewish mysticism. Though published in the 13th century, its teachings are ascribed to R' Shimon ben Yochai of the 2nd century.

ABOUT THE AUTHOR

Rabbi Moshe Becker studied at the Chevron Yeshiva in Givat Mordechai and at The Jerusalem Kollel, receiving *semichah* from Rabbi Yitzchak Berkovits and Rabbi Zalman Nechemia Goldberg. He lectures and writes on topics of Halachah, Jewish history, and Jewish philosophy and has published works in a variety of publications. He currently lives in New York with his family and is a senior analyst at the New York City Department of Education.

ABOUT MOSAICA PRESS

Mosaica Press is an independent publisher of Jewish books. Our authors include some of the most profound, interesting, and entertaining thinkers and writers in the Jewish community today. There is a great demand for high-quality Jewish works dealing with issues of the day — and Mosaica Press is helping fill that need. Our books are available around the world. Please visit us at **www.mosaicapress.com** or contact us at **info@mosaicapress.com**. We will be glad to hear from you.